WEEDS IN THE GARDEN OF WORDS

If the English language is a glorious garden, filled with exotic hybrids and the continuing tradition of heritage specimens, then it is no surprise that we will also find some weeds. Linguistic weeds may have pronunciations we don't want or constructions that are out of place. We may be trying to hold on to words and usage we should perhaps have said farewell to. But as all gardeners know, what one gardener calls a 'weed', another may call a 'flower'. The same goes for words and their usage in English – sometimes we just haven't realized their virtues.

Kate Burridge follows the international success of her book *Blooming English* with another entertaining excursion into the ever-changing nature of our complex and captivating language.

Kate Burridge is Professor of Linguistics at Monash University. She has published widely on English language and linguistics and is well known for her broadcasts on ABC Radio's Soundback.

WEEDS IN THE GARDEN OF WORDS

Further observations on the tangled history of the English language

Kate Burridge

CAMBRIDGE
UNIVERSITY PRESS

CAMBRIDGE UNIVERSITY PRESS
Cambridge, New York, Melbourne, Madrid, Cape Town, Singapore, São Paulo

Cambridge University Press
The Edinburgh Building, Cambridge CB2 2RU, UK

http://www.cambridge.org
Information on this title: www.cambridge.org/9780521853132

First published 2004 by ABC Books for the Australian Broadcasting Corporation
GPO Box 9994, Sydney, NSW 2001, Australia
This edition published in 2005 by
Cambridge University Press. Not for sale in
Australia or New Zealand.

Printed in the United Kingdom at the University Press, Cambridge

A catalogue record for this book is available from the British Library

ISBN-13   978-0-521-85313-2 hardback
ISBN-10   0-521-85313-3 hardback

ISBN-13   978-0-521-61823-6 paperback
ISBN-10   0-521-61823-1 paperback

And unto Adam he said, Because thou hast hearkened unto the voice of thy wife, and hast eaten of the tree, of which I commanded thee, saying, Thou shalt not eat of it: cursed is the ground for thy sake; in sorrow shalt thou eat of it all the days of thy life; Thorns also and thistles shall it bring forth to thee; and thou shalt eat the herb of the field.

Genesis 3:17–18

Contents

Acknowledgments

Weeds in the Garden of Words could not have been written – or at least it would have been a lot harder to write – without the backing of a number of people. First, it is a particular pleasure to thank Susan Morris-Yates at ABC Books and Kate Brett at Cambridge University Press for their help and encouragement. I am also extremely grateful to Suzanne Falkiner for her editorial assistance. Suzanne's insightful comments on everything from budgie smugglers to the intricacies of English punctuation have improved this manuscript immeasurably. Then there are those special friends and colleagues who have supplied support, inspiration and suggestions over the years. Many thanks especially to Amy Williams for helping me with the index and to Allison Pritchard for her valuable comments and examples. To my father, John, I owe a special debt of gratitude for passing on to me from a very early age a love of language and of gardens. His responses to an early version of this book helped me to improve it greatly. As always I must acknowledge an enormous debt to Ross Weber. I have been very fortunate in having his support and encouragement over so many wonderful years. Thank you to Lisa Graham whose care of Daniel gave me the peace of mind that enabled me to finish this book. And, of course, thank you to Daniel – our long walks around Princess Park helped to shape my thoughts on many of the pieces in this book. But it is to the crew at ABC Radio's *Southbank* I am most grateful, for without their continued support there would be no book. Many thanks to Gary Bartholomew, Penny Johnston and Michael Taft. And last (but certainly not least) to ABC listeners I owe a special debt of gratitude. Thank you for those many letters, emails and phone calls – this interest in language is what brings these topics to life and makes my job so rewarding.

Introduction to the Weedy Traits of the English Language

Weeds, as a class, have much in common with criminals. When not engaged in their nefarious activities both may have admirable qualities; a thief may be an affectionate husband and father outside business hours; an aggressive weed in one environment may be a charming wild flower in another.
Sir Edward Salisbury puts it beautifully in the preface to his book
The New Naturalist: Weeds and Aliens.

Weed experts, I gather, have great difficulty coming up with a scientific account of the term *weed*. In my own attempts to come to grips with the concept of the garden weed, I've encountered many different definitions: 'a plant growing where we do not want it'; 'a plant whose virtues are yet to be discovered'; 'a plant growing out of place'; 'a nuisance plant that interferes with human activities'; 'a plant that you do not want'; 'a plant you hate'. More precise definitions, it seems, are impossible – in fact, probably not practicable. The difficulty is that weeds are context specific. It depends entirely on location and on time whether something is classified as a weed or not.

Different soils clearly have different weeds. Some gardeners might spurn a plant that usurps and overgrows their garden. Others may admire that very same plant for its ability to thrive in the impoverished soil of their inner-city courtyard. Lantana, I recall when I was growing up, was much praised for its flowers and its capacity to flourish in neglected gardens. Like that other beautiful 'weed' morning glory, this prickly scrambler provided spectacular camouflage for suburban eyesores – rubbish mounds and rickety fences. Most Australians will also be familiar with the purple flowers

1

of that very pretty agricultural weed *Echium plantagineum*. On one hand, it competes with other plantings and contains alkaloids that can poison cattle. On the other, this attractive 'wildflower' provides purple carpets for tourists to enjoy and produces flowers for nectar when other species can't. Presumably, circumstances dictate what common name this weed goes by – Paterson's curse or salvation Jane. Many people make tea and wine out of that delightful weed, the dandelion. There are even some who grow it as a crop. Scotch (or English) broom is also a glorious-looking pest. Like so many other 'garden escapes', it does particularly well in the pasture land and bushland of North America and Australia. Plants often start off as cherished species – perhaps deliberately introduced as feed plants or garden ornamentals – but over time turn into aggressive weeds. When a prize was awarded to 'prickly pear jam' at the Australasian Botanic and Horticultural Society meeting in Sydney in 1848, *Opuntia stricta* (or common prickly pear) was highly valued as a drought-resistant fodder. But by the 1920s this rampaging menace was invading Queensland and parts of northern New South Wales at a rate of a million acres a year, until finally the cactoblastis moth was introduced to control the infestation. Clearly, many plants are weeds of our own making – we planted them in the first place. And frequently we are also the ones responsible for their success. Humans are among the main agents of weed dispersal. Moreover, many noxious weeds are totally dependent on the conditions and habitats that human activites create.

And so it is with the linguistic weeds that we produce. They often are structural features of the language whose virtues have yet to be realized. They are the pronunciations we don't want, the constructions that are out of place, the words we create but hate. Like weedy plants they are entirely location and time specific. Many of our current *bête noires* are features we overlook or even admire in other languages. I have never, for instance, heard a speaker of English condemn the nasal vowels or dropped consonants of the French language. Double negatives (as in *I don't want no dinner*) are rejected by many as a mark of illiteracy in English; yet double, even multiple negation is a standard attribute of many languages, including French. Features that we revile in the speech of others may well be rampant in our own speech but go completely unnoticed by us (hesitation features such as *umm* and *err*, discourse particles such as *you know*, *yeah-no* and *I mean*).

This kind of doublethink shows up clearly in our confused attitudes towards regional variation. Many of us treasure the English spoken by the Irish and are horrified to learn that the linguistic effects of Irish are some of our current-day weeds, such as *haitch*, *youse* and *growun* (for 'grown'). Many enjoy the invariant tags of the Welsh ('They do good work, isn't it'), the l-dropping of the Scottish (*fou* 'full' and *saut* 'salt'), and their glottal stops (*wa'er* and *bu'er* for 'water' and 'butter') but despise these very same features when they appear on our own doorstep. Most of us, it seems, admire the linguistic features characteristic of picturesque and unspoiled rural parts of the English-speaking world. But often these are precisely the same features that we condemn in the regional dialects of heavily industrialized urban centres – the quaint rustic forms that make us go weak at the knees suddenly become bad and ugly-sounding.

Over time, too, the status of linguistic features can change strikingly. Words such as *aint* and *gotten* once flourished in the language of some of our finest writers. Something happened, and they fell from linguistic grace. Expressions at one time adored by speakers are often abandoned by those same speakers – overuse renders them a weedy cliché. The days are already numbered for some of our current vogue expressions – *absolutely, no worries, bottom line*. I'm sure there are many you would like to see eradicated. Even grammatical weeds are totally centred around human value judgements and these change with time. An exuberance of negative expressions (two, three, perhaps even more negators in a sentence) was a prized feature of Old and Middle English; yet, as earlier described, double negation has become the bane of many speakers today. Prized pronunciations can suddenly come to the attention of speakers and become irksome – sometime during the 18th century h-dropping, g-dropping, once posh, became scoffed at.

On the other hand, time can witness linguistic weeds turning into prized garden ornamentals. American linguist Geoffrey Nunberg describes how Benjamin Franklin once wrote to dictionary maker Noah Webster to try to convince him to 'set a discountenancing mark' upon the verb *to notice* and the use of *improve* in place of *ameliorate*. It's hard for us to understand what possible objections Franklin could have had to these verbs. Both *notice* and *improve* are thoroughly respectable today. And so it is that many of our current irritating colloquialisms, sloppy pronunciations, errors of grammar, new-fangled meanings and slangy expressions will end up being part of the repertoire of Standard English in the future. Today's weeds can become tomorrow's respected and rewarding species.

'Magnificent constitutions'

Few plants, when they are young and newly planted, can compete successfully with weeds, which have the advantages of enormous vigour, drought resistance, few diseases and, in many cases, the ability to produce anti-growth substances to fetter the development of other plants.

Peter Cundall *Seasonal Tasks for the Practical Australian Gardener* 1989

I was crestfallen to see that the thriving (and therefore much-loved) plants in my own garden all featured prominently in Suzanne Ermert's *Gardener's Companion to Weeds*, most notably the white arum lily and the seaside daisy. That my blue periwinkle invaded and smothered all adjacent plantings I attributed to my gardening prowess – but there it was on page 164. There's clearly another aspect to weeds. They are highly successful. A component of *The Macquarie Dictionary* definition of *weed* is 'grows profusely'. Weeds, it turns out, share certain biological features that enable them to prosper. They have prolific and effective seed production and dispersal mechanisms, or they spread by rhizomes and tubers (which means they can regenerate from the smallest of fragments), and they're often unpalatable to browsers. In short, they are very, very hard to kill. As Vita Sackville-West describes them, 'all appear to be possessed of magnificent constitutions'.

One of the challenges confronting linguists is to determine the conditions that allow linguistic weeds to prosper in a particular language at a particular time. For example, sounds naturally drop from the ends of words and English has experienced massive erosion of this kind. This has coincided with a complete overhaul of its grammar. All our close linguistic relatives are experiencing these same changes, but at different times and at different rates. Why? And why, within one language system, do some weeds end up flourishing while others eventually wither? For instance, language change is typically marked by rivalry between different forms. So what are the capabilities that enable one feature to be triumphant and spread through the language? Hundreds of slang expressions are created by speakers each year. Most fall by the wayside but some succeed – why? Pronunciations such as 'shoo' and 'shooter' for *sue* and *suitor* were denounced in the 17th century as 'barbarous'. They were eventually eradicated. So how come *sugar* and *sure* (pronounced today as 'shooger' and 'shaw') snuck through the controls? And what enables certain linguistic weeds to extend their perimeters beyond one social group to spread to others? Many of the grammatical weeds I describe in this book are everywhere. Features such as irregular verb forms (*seen* in place of *saw* and *done* in place of *did*), plural forms of the pronoun 'you' (*youse, you-all, you-uns*) and *never* as a general negator crop up in non-standard varieties all over the English-speaking world.

The weed image raises an obvious question. Clearly there are truly nasty plants out there that pose serious environmental threats. But do our linguistic weeds ever have a truly detrimental effect on the landscapes they infest? They can be pesky, it's true. Weedy words can be distracting to people, and if they are distracting, they interfere with effective communication. As you well know, linguistic features that offend or irritate (for whatever reason) become particularly salient. You might suddenly notice the chap you're speaking with says 'yeah-no' a lot of the time and it's starting to irk. Suddenly, all you can hear is the repetition of this disagreeable phrase. Meaning shifts, too, can occasionally cause misunderstandings at the time they're occurring. What does that person mean by 'next Saturday' or 'a couple of bread rolls'? What's more, linguistic weeds can even disrupt the language system by introducing complexity and anomaly elsewhere in the language. Pronunciation changes, for example, often mess up the grammar. But while linguistic weeds are bothersome, they're rarely truly pernicious.

So another challenge for linguists is to discover why it is that certain features become irritating to speakers. Certainly, many of our linguistic weeds represent recent developments in the language, and speakers are generally suspicious of the new. Yet many neologisms sneak in unnoticed, and many exist for some time, only later to attract adverse attention. There are pronunciations, for example, that many today condemn as sloppy – 'ashoom' for *assume* and 'prezhoom' for *presume*, for instance. No one has yet, as far as I know, commented on a similar pronunciation change that is currently turning *tree* into 'chree' and *street* into 'shtreet'. The little marker *yeah-no* had been in Australian English for a good while before it started to crawl under the skin of some speakers. Why only now has it become such a source of irritation? Really, all this has little to do with the language as such, but with what is at stake socially. The significance of language usage derives from its cultural and social setting, and our squeamishness about certain words, pronunciations and grammar arises accordingly. Many encounter *yeah-no* for the first time in television and radio sports interviews, especially where competitors are being interviewed following a win. The expression occurs particularly often with younger, less experienced interviewees. Perhaps it is these associations with sports-speak that have now rendered *yeah-no* a weed for some.

Classifying weeds

One of the prettiest weeds that we have in our modern garden, and which alternates between being our greatest joy and our greatest torment, is the Welsh Poppy. It succeeds so well in this dry soil that it sows itself everywhere; but when it stands up, with its profusion of yellow flowers well above its bed of bright green leaves, in some fortunate situation where it can not only be spared, but encouraged and admired, it is a real pleasure.

Mrs C W Earle
Pot-Pourri from a Surrey Garden 1897

Classifying weedy plants, I gather, is a tricky business. There is no one category – be it habitat, growth behaviour, morphology, life history – that will do for all plants in the weed flora. I have chosen to classify these linguistic weeds straightforwardly according to habitat; in other words, where they reside in the language system. The book therefore organizes these weeds into three main groups – 'lexical weeds', 'the weeds in sounds and spelling' and 'grammatical weeds'. These headings are handy but not entirely accurate. Like all our linguistic labels they give the impression of easily identifiable and neatly compartmentalized entities. However, such tidy classifications are never the reality and you'll find there is some overlap.

Your reactions to these weeds will be interesting. It's true, I have organized the pieces into these sections for convenience, but also because we do react differently to linguistic weeds depending on where they live. With most speakers, I find, there is a continuum of tolerance. People appear to feel far more generous towards weeds within vocabulary than to those that inhabit our sounds and spelling. And weedy tendencies in grammar, it seems, attract the fiercest condemnation of all. Finally, you may find yourself surprised at the inclusion of some of the linguistic specimens here. This is to be expected. The expression 'weed' is, after all, anthropocentric – we view something as a weed in terms of our own experiences and values. As I mentioned earlier, the garden weeds in my *Companion to Weeds* include some of my most cherished possessions. And so it is with our linguistic weeds. They are totally centred upon the bees that are in our bonnets.

Just a final note on the organization of this book. Like its parent, *Blooming English*, *Weeds in the Garden of Words* is meant for dipping into, and this can be done at any point. Even though they might deal with related themes, the individual pieces are all self-contained. Let me also emphasize that these pieces were originally written to be read aloud on radio. They are therefore chatty, informal and probably in style resemble something closer to speech than to writing. They have no footnotes or endnotes. However, at the end of the book I have provided a bibliography detailing the authors I have cited. The list includes works of literature, of linguistics, and of course of gardening: the books that have inspired me – most notably *The Illustrated Virago Book of Women Gardeners* and Peter Cundall's *Seasonal Tasks for the Practical Australian Gardener*, which supplied many wonderful quotations.

Backdrop – standard languages and gardens

I cannot lay too great stress upon the neatness in which a lady's garden should be kept. If it is not beautifully neat, it is nothing. For this reason, keep every plant distinct in the flower-beds; let every tall flower be well staked, that the wind may not blow it prostrate; rake away dead leaves from the beds, and trim every flower-root from discoloured leaves, weeds, &c.; remove all weeds and stones the moment they appear, and clear away decaying stems, which are so littering and offensive to the eye. There is always some employment of this kind for every week in the year.
Marie E. Jackson *The Florist's Manual* 1822

The story of English is a tangled history of nature and human activity – the endless tussle between, on one hand, 'the boundless chaos of a living speech' (as Samuel Johnson put it in the preface to his dictionary) and, on the other, Standard English, the variety that has been created over the years by the prescriptive endeavours of people such as Samuel Johnson.

Standard languages represent a kind of linguistic 'best practice' – a set of behaviours that claims to excel all others. Correctness, precision, purity, elegance are the perceived qualities of the standard. It is the measure of excellence – the 'benchmark', if you like, against which we gauge all other varieties of the language. Standard English is promoted in schools and used in law courts and government institutions; students use it in essays; broadcasters speak it on radio (although these days this requirement is sometimes relaxed); instructors teach it to foreign students of English. Speakers are somehow expected to acquire its rules and those that don't are often regarded as recalcitrant, lazy, even incompetent. They are said to have poor grammar – or worse, no grammar at all. You'll notice that we even call this privileged variety 'the standard language' and not 'the standard dialect'. Since dialects are held to be substandard varieties of a language – varieties not quite up to scratch – the label 'standard dialect' would seem a kind of self-contradiction. For many people Standard English *is* English. What they think of as the rules of English grammar are the rules of this one

8

variety – more especially, in fact, its written form. Words aren't somehow real until they appear in a dictionary. People often ask whether something they've heard, or even used themselves, is an actual word or not. Use isn't enough to qualify something as language.

Bounding and cultivation

Large or small, the garden should look both orderly and rich. It should be well fenced from the outer world. It should by no means imitate either the wilfulness or the wildness of Nature.
William Morris *Hopes and Fears for Art* 1883

Standard English is a variety that has been artificially constructed over many, many years, not by any English Language Academy (because there hasn't been one), but by a network of different groups, including writers of style guides and usage manuals, dictionary makers, editors, teachers and newspaper columnists. Over the years their cleaning-up activities have amassed an arsenal of prescriptive texts that have gone to promote and legitimise a single fixed and approved variety. These dictionaries, grammars and handbooks record, regulate, tidy up and iron out. Their neat lists, elegant definitions and fine-spun paradigms necessarily ignore the 'wilfulness' and 'wildness' that are part of the diversity and variability necessary for a language system to thrive.

Standard English is in fact a recent arrival on the linguistic scene. Standard languages have to be nurtured, and from the time of Old English, around a thousand years ago, until the late Middle Ages, the language existed with very little attention paid to it at all. Certainly, there was one dialect of Old English known as West Saxon that did have a bit of an edge over the others, but this is not, however, the predecessor of our modern standard. To begin with, its career was cut short by the arrival of the French in 1066. For several centuries after the Norman Conquest, English was well and truly under the Norman French thumb. French and Latin were the languages of power, and when people wrote it was typically in these languages. Eventually when writers started writing in English again, they did it in their local variety, using home-grown forms and spellings. And most important, there was no single prestige model that people were under pressure to follow. There were no dictionaries, no grammars, no spelling books, and variation was rampant. People's attitude to English also reveals it was a long way from being standardized. They didn't think of it as entirely respectable, so when it came to serious literature they continued to use Latin.

But things gradually changed. By the late medieval period the dialect used in and around London was starting to get the upper hand. From the early 1400s those in King Henry V's court began corresponding in English, and much of the business of government at this time was conducted in 'King's English'. It's important to emphasise that the success of the London dialect wasn't because of any linguistic advantage it had over other contenders. It wasn't a conscious choice. When varieties come to dominate in this way, it's not for linguistic reasons. London English piggybacked on a series of geographical, cultural, economic and political episodes. These included the emergence of London as a political and commercial centre and its proximity to Oxford and Cambridge; Chaucer's literary genius; and William Caxton's first printing presses in Westminster – these had the combined effect of putting London English in such a position that standardization was inevitable. If a city other than London had possessed the same non-linguistic advantages (let's say York), the dialect of that region would have spread in the same way. And how different Standard English would be today!

It was during the 16th century that English really began to take off. Suddenly people started to talk about the language in regard to its grammar, vocabulary and writing. And there were clues that standardization was just around the corner, for they also began to talk about their language in a more judgemental fashion. Sure, people had been making judgements about other people's speech for centuries. Observations on regional varieties were commonplace, but now for the first time we find a real vocabulary of abuse. On one hand, there was the right sort of language (described as 'pure', 'natural') and, on the other, the wrong kind (described as 'corrupt', 'false'). These labels hint at the concept of an approved standard – to stray away from this ideal was to stray away from what was pure and good. But it still took until well into the 18th century before English truly ousted Latin as the language of learned and technical writing. In the preface to his 1653 *Grammar of the English Language*, John Wallis wrote of how the importance of English had driven him to write a grammar. I should add that Wallis had chosen to write his grammar in Latin. Poor old English still wasn't quite up to the task!

Clearly, gardens and standard languages have much in common. Both are human constructions and they share two fundamental characteristics. They are restricted by boundaries and they are also cultivated. Prescriptive endeavours have left Standard English regularized and homogenized – bound. There is no room for variation. There is no room for options. Speakers cannot vacillate between *lie* and *lay* or *I done it* and *I did it*. Only one choice carries the stamp of approval. We are looking here at a kind of linguistic monolith with a fixed set of strict rules and conventions that now defines linguistic 'best practice'. It is an ideal we have for our language, and everyday usage will never quite come up to scratch. Even speakers and writers whose language comes closest to 'best practice' frequently violate the rules of the Standard – probably because the Standard is, in a sense, too correct. Constructions like *Whom did you see at the party?* and *The data are misleading* are simply too pernickety for many speakers, even for formal occasions.

Indeed, the creators of the Standard themselves do not always observe their own prescriptions. Later in this book I look at some of the recommendations of one of the very early codifiers, Bishop Lowth. His *Short Introduction to English Grammar* (1762) was one of the first grammars of English. Lowth was very clear in the grammatical rules he laid down. Yet, in his own private correspondence, he constantly flouted these rules. It's not clear what motivated his choices here. Perhaps his recommendations were inappropriately formal for his intimate letters. But the point is that language is simply not amenable to being forced into perfect standard moulds, and anyone who attempts to do so will undoubtedly find themselves in as contradictory a position as Lowth did. Prescriptive endeavours necessarily promote a kind of mental dishonesty – either self-deception or full-blown hypocrisy.

Speech communities are extremely complex and language has to cover a huge range of social behaviour. Yet, variability and mutability – qualities intrinsic to any linguistic system – do not sit happily within the classifications of a pure and consistent standard variety. The label 'standard' entails not only 'best practice' but also 'uniform practice' and this is only practical in the context of the written language, especially formal written language. To adapt William Morris' description of the garden, it's the written language that we can fence off from the outer world. The writing process (and the conscious self-censorship that accompanies it) has a straitjacketing effect that safeguards the language to some extent from 'the boundless chaos of a living speech' – in other words, the flux and variance that is the reality of language. And in a sense it's our dependence on, and veneration for, the written word that now blinds us to this reality.

The garden is never static

> ... *perhaps the chiefest attraction of a garden is that occupation can always be found there.*
> Alicia Amherst, *Children's Gardens* 1902

Clearly writers of dictionaries and grammars are going to be in an impossible position here. In their book on English words, linguists Stockwell and Minkova describe how many fine dictionaries such as *Funk and Wagnall's* have now dropped by the wayside because they didn't update. People simply stopped using them. And yet if the dictionary makers and handbook writers do acknowledge current usage, howls erupt about declining educational standards. As one outraged citizen put it after the appearance of Webster's *Third New International Dictionary* in 1961: 'If a sentry forsakes his post and places an army in danger, the penalty is severe. If a guardian ceases to guard and neglects his duty to children, there are few who would not condemn. If a great dictionary forsakes its post as the guardian of our language, how can one avoid disappointment?' (cited in Preston 2002, p. 149)

People clearly have faith in the idea of linguistic perfection, in the notion that a language should be uniform and consistent – and they want their reference books to tell them what is and what is not correct usage. Dictionaries and handbooks that acknowledge change are seen to be abdicating their responsibility. So too are style manuals that recognise other options. But linguistic systems are never static and dictionaries and handbooks must reflect this to stay current. Take the collision in Antipodean English of the two verbs *bring* and *buy* – increasingly *bought* is appearing as the past of *bring* (instead of *brought*). Certainly these are early days, but the fact that *bought* now sometimes appears in print as the past of *bring* suggests the change is well and truly entrenched. Yet it would be a brave editor who takes this new usage on board. Of course, no one cares these days that *go* has filched its past tense *went* from *wend*. No one worries that the most common verb – the verb *to be* – is a mixture of four different verbs – *was/were* (from Old English *wesan*); *is/am* (from the verbal root *es*-); *are* (from *er*-); and *be* (from Old English *beon*). This is one linguistic mongrel! Standard English will eventually have to embrace the mixed pedigree of *bring* too – that is, if it survives.

Linguists are also clearly in an impossible position. I recall the time a new style guide for English appeared on the scene. In a discussion on radio with the writer Kim Lockwood, I suggested that the rules he outlined weren't cut-and-dried and that he should have guided his readers through the range of available options. Other rules, I argued, were no longer valid and should be dispensed with. One frustrated talkback caller summed me up – 'She doesn't get it, does she?' And that caller was right. There is a sense in which we linguists definitely don't get it. It doesn't matter what linguistic science says. Speakers of English believe in a standard language. They believe in, if not the existence, then the possibility of a totally regular and homogenous language system. And such beliefs are powerful – as anyone who has tried to mess with the cherished standard knows. Yet we are going to have to mess with this cherished standard if we are to develop a better and more constructive public discourse on language. To create a standard language or to build a garden is to enter into a partnership with natural processes. Languages and gardens are never finished products.

Our Lexical Weeds: the World of Jargon, Slang and Euphemism

*Some time ago I blundered once again . . . You see, it
happened while I was sowing the last of the seeds in a row
of peas. As I bent to retrieve some I had dropped, there in
front of my horrified eyes, was a small clump of oxalis.
How this dreadful weed had sneaked into the garden in
spite of all my precautions will never be known, but there
it was, deceptively pretty, a tiny cluster of soft green,
shamrock leaves. That's when the awful mistake was made.
I should have dropped everything and dug it out straight
away, in a perfectly normal blind panic, but I didn't.*
Peter Cundall *Seasonal Tasks for the Practical Australian
Gardener* 1989

Language of special groups

Someone at the University of Melbourne kindly emailed me about
the recent seizure by ordinary language of a number of specialist
expressions. In particular, he drew my attention to the terms *epicentre* and *ballistic*. What disturbed this person was not so much the
fact that the wider community was taking up these terms, but the
misuse of them. *Epicentre*, as he pointed out, is a term from geology. In its technical meaning it refers to the true centre of a disturbance – the point from which earthquake waves go out. These days
in ordinary language it seems to be acquiring a more general sense
of simply 'middle'. The ABC news, for example, reported the arrest
of someone described as being at 'the epicentre of a drug ring'. This
usage is indeed new – it hasn't yet made it into the dictionary, but
presumably our dictionary makers are all watching it with interest.

The term *ballistic*, on the other hand, is a little more complicated. Certainly the noun *ballistics* is a technical term meaning 'the science of the motion of items such as bullets, bombs and rockets'. *Ballistic* then pertains to the throwing of projectiles. Its colloquial use in the phrase *to go ballistic* is a colourful one and has been in the language for some time now. This one has made it into the dictionary. Of course *to go ballistic* suggests someone has exploded with rage, but as these emails pointed out, when missiles go ballistic they don't explode; they actually coast. Ballistic missiles, if I understand correctly, are powered only when ascending, and then they free-fall; in other words, they coast after the initial force that propels them ceases. So the colloquialism *to go ballistic* hasn't quite got it right. And this is typical of what happens when specialist terms enter everyday language. Usually the words end up drifting a long way from their original precise definitions as they expand into more and more contexts. Look at what happened to *quantum leap*. In its technical sense it still means 'the sudden transition of an atom or electron from one energy state to another'. I don't know much about atoms or electrons, but this *quantum leap* certainly doesn't suggest much of a leap at all. In general usage, of course, *quantum leaps* are substantial, but since leaps generally do involve considerable movement and speed, it's hardly surprising that we've arrived at this meaning.

Ordinary language is always filching terms from specialist languages in this way. We might complain about jargon but the fact is, it can be useful. Much jargon is efficient and economical and it often captures distinctions that aren't made in ordinary language. Just look at the transfer of computer jargon into our everyday parlance. *Information overload* can happen to us all. People *interface* and *network* on a regular basis now. Linguistics lecturers can even be *user-friendly*. In each case, the original narrow specification has been lost and the term has expanded its meaning. Words also wear out through use. They become mundane. So speakers are always on the lookout for newer and more exciting ways of saying something. Let's face it, *epicentre* packs more of a punch than *centre*.

Of course, I can understand people's concerns when terms from their professions are appropriated in this way. I can't say I'm terribly chuffed about the way the word *semantics* gets bandied about in everyday usage. But it's difficult to talk about misuse when ordinary language chooses to adopt a term-of-art like *epicentre* or *ballistic*. Ordinary language has always borrowed from jargon, just as jargon has always borrowed from ordinary language. And each beats the new terms into a different shape to suit its needs. It's always been this way.

Networks and glitches

 When everyday language swipes words from specialist languages the effect is usually a broadening of definition. The original narrow specification is lost and the term expands its meaning. However, when jargons filch their specialist terms from everyday language, this generally has the effect of narrowing the meaning – the words come to mean less than they did before. Many of the terms that earmark computer-speak these days actually derive from common usage in exactly this way. The verb *input* dates back to Middle English, when it had the general meaning 'to put on'. For example, in the Wyclif Bible of 1382 we can read in Acts 28, Verse 3 how 'Poul hade gederid sum multitude of kittingis of vynes, and ynputt on the fyer' (in other words, Paul had gathered a bundle of twigs, and input them [= laid them] on the fire). *Networks* were works of netted threads or wires centuries before they linked computers together (of course they affiliated radio or television stations before this). *Interface* comes from a 19th-century noun meaning generally 'a surface where two portions of matter or space meet'. *Glitch* 'slippery place' entered English from Yiddish and was used in electronics well before it was picked up by the computer industry to refer to a 'bug' or 'small problem'. It's interesting that these terms are now re-entering common usage and being generalized from their specialized computer senses. *Glitches* now occur in all sorts of places, not just computer programs. Sometimes the meaning changes are remarkable. A *hacker* was (not surprisingly) a person who hacked things – the word was used for cut-throats and bullies. Nowadays it refers to someone who breaks into computer systems (or, for some people, to any computer-programming enthusiast).

New conversions

One remarkable aspect of English is its ability to convert words into other parts of speech without adding any kind of ending or prefix. It's a very easy way English speakers have of expanding their vocabulary. We have the noun *stretcher*, for instance. If you wanted to briefly describe a football player being carried off the field on a stretcher, you might make use of this handy linguistic device to simply say, *They are going to stretcher him off the field*. This is something known as conversion. In this case a noun has been converted to a verb. It's also sometimes called zero-derivation, because you're deriving a new word by not really doing anything at all. You can take a verb like *reprieve* and turn it into a noun by adding *-al*, as in *a reprieval*, or you could simply make it a noun – *a reprieve*.

Typically, conversion involves the major word classes like nouns, verbs, adjectives and adverbs. The most common conversions appear to be from verb to noun – for instance *a guess, a call, a command*, and more recently *a think, a read*, and of course *a big ask*. We also have plenty of nouns being changed to verbs, for example *to bottle, to bridge, to mail*, and more recently *to trash, to network, to impact (on)* and *to leaflet*. There are also adjectives changing to verbs, such as *to better, to empty, to open*, and more recently *to total*, as in *totalling a car*. Adjectives to nouns include *a roast, a weekly, a regular*, and more recently *a given, a nasty*. There don't appear to be any restrictions on conversion – words can move between classes with extraordinary ease.

Among conversions from the minor, more grammatical word classes are *up* and *down*, which can be much more than just simple prepositions. We have, for instance, *to up the stakes* and *to down tools*. We can also be *on the up* or *have a down on someone*. Something can be *up-market* or *a down experience* and we can *set up* or *get up* – or *down* for that matter. Even sentence linkers like *but* can convert into other parts of speech, as in the jocular phrase *but me no buts*. I imagine obscenities are among the most grammatically flexible of all. Slang is very good at taking an obscene verb and turning it into a different part of speech for a bit more colour.

Conversion is something we've been doing in the language for centuries. It's not a new trend by any means and we have a multitude of words that have been created in this way. Curiously, it's a convenience not all speakers fully appreciate. I remember the outcry when one sporting commentator reported *Well, it wasn't gold, but at least he medalled.* A more conservative speaker may find such individual inventiveness abhorrent, and many are quick to condemn even everyday usages like *have a listen* and *to stretcher.* Complaints about new conversions are commonplace, and always have been. When the verb *to contact* was created from the noun and first entered general usage, it was considered hideous jargon and faced fierce resistance. *The Oxford English Dictionary* has a small entry for it, with usages such as this one from the 1930s: 'A charming lady in the publicity business shocked me when we parted by saying "It has been such fun contacting you".' Such appalling language, and from 'a charming lady', what's more!

I googled him

 Google is the name of one of the most powerful search engines available on the World Wide Web (www.google.com). Its success is demonstrated by the recent appearance of the new verb *to google.* To say something like 'I googled him' or 'I googled it' means that you used the Google site to search for information on a certain person or thing. How much more convenient this is than the long-winded 'I did a Google search on him'. Apparently, the verb is even showing signs of generalizing its meaning. Some speakers, I'm told, now use it to refer to any search, not simply a Google search, and I am grateful to Allison Pritchard for alerting me to it. New conversions often come to my attention when someone complains about them, but so far people have been quiet on this one.

New words

In June 2003, Collins announced the appearance of its new *Essential English Dictionary*. The publicity material proudly described how this recent edition sets 'new standards in clarity, accessibility and practical help'. Included were a whole range of new entries, too – dialect words like *baffies*, a Scots word for 'slippers'; Harry Potter-inspired creations such as *quidditch* and *muggle*; some clever neologisms from the world of business such as *aesthetic labour*, an expression that apparently refers to 'the hiring of employees for their appearance or accent in order to enhance the image of a company'; and – one of my favourites – *greenwash* 'a superficial or insincere display of concern for the environment that is shown by an organisation'. There were also quite a number of new entries that one might think border on slang, if not sit smack dab in middle of it – words like *bootylicious* to describe a woman with an attractive rear, *beer goggles* for fuzzy vision after too much alcohol, and *bada bing* as an exclamation that indicates something will happen predictably and without effort. There were even SMS abbreviations like *ATB* 'all the best' and *A3* meaning 'anytime, anywhere, any place'. In fact, there were something like 5,500 new words in this dictionary. And not everyone was happy.

Many people see makers of dictionaries and style manuals as guardians of the language and arbiters of linguistic goodness. Their publications safeguard the language against 'the boundless chaos of a living speech', to quote Samuel Johnson again. Johnson had produced in 1755 what was really the first complete dictionary of English. And his intentions were quite clear – to banish what he described as 'barbarous corruptions', 'licentious idioms' and 'colloquial barbarisms'. I'm not sure he would have approved of *bootylicious* or *beer goggles*. He most certainly would have slapped on a label identifying such usage as barbarous or low, if he included them at all. And here, of course, is the problem. The entries labelled as unfit for general use in Johnson's dictionary were words like *abominably*, *nowadays*, *bamboozle* and the adjective *novel* – all wholly respectable today.

Clearly the 'boundless chaos of a living speech' won't go away. In fact Samuel Johnson himself recognised this as soon as he had produced his dictionary. He wrote at length about the futility of trying to 'fix' the language or 'ascertain' it, as he put it. Centuries later Robert Burchfield, as editor of *The Oxford English Dictionary*, described English as 'a fleet of juggernaut trucks that goes on regardless'. As he pointed out, no amount of linguistic intervention can prevent the cycle of changes that lies ahead. Clearly, compiling dictionaries is a tricky business. Vocabulary is the most unstable aspect of a language and dictionary makers are constantly having to redraw the admission and exclusion boundary for marginal vocabulary items. *Yeah-no* is a new discourse marker in a number of varieties of English. So when will it appear in our dictionaries? For most of us *To beg the question* means 'to raise the question'. When will our dictionaries acknowledge this meaning?

Nipplegate

I was delighted when I heard on ABC radio a number of references to *nipplegate*. I was beginning to worry that, despite *zippergate*, *peckergate* and *fornigate* (after the Clinton–Starr conflict), *-gate* words might be on the way out. *Nipplegate*, of course, referred to Janet Jackson's little stunt in early February 2004. Mid-show, at half-time during the Super Bowl match, Justin Timberlake ripped open Jackson's rather peculiar-looking bustier to reveal a right breast equipped with a silver nipple ornament. 'A wardrobe malfunction' was the explanation. A likely story, given the chic silver sunburst she just happened to be wearing at the time. The press smelled a rat – hence, *nipplegate*. Words ending in *-gate* usually tell a story of jiggery-pokery and hanky-panky. The original *-gate* was, as we know, *Watergate*, after the apartment–office complex where the events leading to Richard Nixon's downfall unfolded. This symbol for political scandal subsequently sprouted a whole heap of *-gates* such as *Dianagate*, *travelgate*, *papergate* and *prisongate*.

The word *nipplegate* and all these other *-gates* involve a blending of two words with some kind of segment in common.

Sometimes they're called *portmanteau* words. This is a label we owe to Lewis Carroll, who first used the term to describe the lexical inventions in his poem *Jabberwocky* – wonderful creations such as *slithy*, *mimsy* and *galumph*. 'Portmanteau' is now a rather old-fashioned expression for a suitcase with a number of compartments, but it nicely captures the packing-up of multiple meanings into single words. They can be very expressive and often extremely witty, too.

Certainly since the 1970s blending has really taken off as a way of creating new and exciting words. In addition to the *greenwash* mentioned earlier, we now have *explorenography*, 'tourism in exotic and dangerous places', *ecotourism* 'tourism designed not to degrade the environment', *advertorial* 'a newspaper article which has been paid for by an advertiser' and *cocacolonization*, an expression that beautifully conjures up American economic imperialism. The development of the Internet has given rise to a whole spate of clever punning blends – there's a special Internet etiquette now referred to as *netiquette*; *spamouflage*, a deceptive 'non-spam-like header on a spam email message'; *pagejacking*, an Internet scam whereby porn operators clone legitimate web pages. And then there's something I suffer from on a regular basis – *compfusion*, 'computer induced confusion'.

Some portmanteau words become so widespread they give rise to new affixes. In fact, a word like *nipplegate* probably shouldn't be described as a portmanteau any more. So popular are the words derived from *Watergate* that they've sprouted a new ending: *-gate*. So that's the tricky thing – when can we say we have a new affix? For instance, there are words like *edutainment* and *infotainment*. If more such blends appear I can imagine a new *-tainment* ending emerging, in the spirit of the *-oholic* suffix in words such as *chocaholic* and *sleepaholic*. The mother blend here was *workaholic*.

Yeah-no, I reckon he's a good bloke

One fairly new arrival on the linguistic scene is the curious phrase *yeah-no*. It's currently rampant in the Antipodes, especially Australia and New Zealand, and I understand it has recently been detected in the UK. You've perhaps heard the expression and maybe even wondered about it – surely speakers are contradicting themselves when they say *yeah* immediately followed by *no*? But agreement and disagreement frequently co-occur in our conversations. Anglo culture generally goes in for non-hostile interaction. The emphasis is on harmony, with a preference for agreement. In short, we are conventionally polite, whatever we're feeling deep down. *Yeah-no* forms part of our repertoire of politeness strategies, but like most of its discourse relatives (such as *I mean, you know, I think, like*), it seems to have a range of different functions. My colleague Margaret Florey and I have been delving into what some of these functions might be for Australian English and here's what we have discovered so far. As you'll see, *yeah-no* has important duties, both to do with creating cohesive conversation and with the more pragmatic function of expressing a speaker's feelings and attitudes.

One use for *yeah-no* relates to straightforward disagreement and agreement, as in 'Yeah-no, I'd rather take the *fromage frais*' (my response to a shop assistant's suggestion that I buy ricotta cheese instead). So why appear to agree when in fact you're about to disagree? Well, you don't want to be seen to contradict, so you diminish the threat by making a positive evaluation first, then following it with a negative one. I wanted *fromage frais* and my rejection of ricotta cheese was attenuated by an initial *yeah-no*. To simply say 'No' would be too blunt. My reply *yeah-no* minimized the impression of disagreement. Someone asked me once, 'Would you object to that?' My answer was 'Yeah-no'; in other words, 'No, I wouldn't object'. So I was actually in agreement with that person. But there's clearly potential for misunderstanding with a bare *no*.

Another related function of *yeah-no* is as a strengthened *yes*. You hear this expressive *yeah-no* where the agreement is emphatic. Here's another actual example: Someone said, 'He had a good time up there, didn't he?' The reply was, 'Yeah-no – he had an absolute ball'. It's curious, isn't it, how *no* can reinforce *yes*, but it does. The effect of *no* here is to knock on the head any possibility of contradiction – any imaginary remark or thought that might raise doubts. This is lively agreement.

Yeah-no has yet another role in our conversations which is more a linking or orientation role. What it does is create relevance between the turns of a conversation. What you often find is that *yeah* acknowledges the previous statement but *no* resumes a topic that preceded it in the conversation. Here's an example. Two women were talking about a concert on television. Then one of the speakers took the conversation off on a bit of tangent with talk of taping the concert. The second speaker then said, 'Yeah-no, it was really good'. Here she was acknowledging what the previous speaker had said, even though she wanted to revert to the earlier topic of just how good the concert was. Like so many of these markers, *yeah-no* strengthens rapport with the hearer. It indicates interest or support.

There is also a use of *yeah-no* that relates more to the speaker and is more personal. It's a kind of hedging expression, one that somehow tempers the force of what's being said. One context where you often hear this personal *yeah-no* is when someone has been complimented. It is rampant in sporting conversations. My colleague Margaret is a sports buff and has collected many examples. For instance, interviewer Tim Bailey compliments Ky Hurst (winner of 'One Summer' Ironman competition at Coolangatta in 1999): ' … and with me is one champion, a phenomenal effort, Ky Hurst. You said you felt buoyant today, you proved that. Some of the best body-surfing we've ever seen'. Ky Hurst replies with a 'yeah-no' – *yeah* acknowledges the compliment (not to do so would seem ungrateful) and the following *no* effectively softens its impact. He continues his speech with a battery of hedging expressions such as 'pretty', 'I think', 'you know', finally attributing his achievement to the excellent beach conditions. In Anglo-Australian culture it is considered unacceptable to skite or stand out and there is a social obligation to downplay the impact of a compliment. A person who has been complimented experiences pressure to accept the comment graciously, but at the same time to appear to be modest.

Now, it's true we often sneer at these markers, mistaking them for hesitation noises like *er* and *umm*. But these are in no way meaningless little expressions that speakers use to fill in time while they're thinking. They are mind-bogglingly complex and their meanings can be excruciatingly difficult to figure out. I've barely touched on *yeah-no* here. And bear in mind I haven't mentioned the variants of *yeah-no* – there's *yeah well no, yeah but no, yep nuh, yes no no* and many others – not to mention *no yeah* and all its different versions!

The earworm and the injured liverwurst

When Collins announced its new *Essential English Dictionary* I was delighted to see that among its 5,500 new entries was that wonderful word *earworm*. This is an expression I've been using for many years now to describe that really annoying little bit of music that rattles around inside one's head, sometimes for days on end. It's catchy, it's irritating and it just won't go away. *Earworm* is actually a word I'd swiped from the German language – English simply didn't have a word for this concept and *earworm* (or *Ohrwurm*) captured the idea beautifully, I thought. And now I see from the new Collins dictionary that we've borrowed it officially.

In fact, technically, *earworm* is not a borrowing, since what we've done is swipe the German idiom and render it totally into English. Such things are known as *calques* or *loan translations* and we have a lot of them in English – a number from German too. For instance, the wine *Cold Duck* is a loan translation of German *Kalte Ente* (originally this expression referred to the leftover wine that got mixed and drunk at the end of a party, a folk remodelling of *Kalte Ende* 'cold ends'). When we translate foreign expressions in this way, we are creating new idioms for the language.

As I've mentioned previously, our English language is something of a lexical bitser (or mongrel), with around seventy-five per cent of its vocabulary filched from other languages. More than 120 languages, in fact, have contributed to our lexical coffers. German words make up only a small proportion of this lexical loot. And yet there are some significant items among them – everyday terms like *delicatessen, kindergarten, rucksack, poodle, gimmick, waltz, dunk,* and of course items of food and drink like *noodle, pretzel, lager, pumpernickel, sauerkraut, schnitzel, frankfurter* – and don't forget *hamburger*. Most of these lexical aliens, you'll notice, have been totally naturalized – beaten into shape to suit the English sound system. But some German loans retain more of their Germanness. We've adopted but not adapted them, or at least not yet adapted them. Among the drink terms are *kirsch* and *schnapps*, for example.

German has contributed a few lexical curiosities too. When a person sneezes, someone often answers *gesundheit*. Most of us would exclaim *ouch* if we hit our thumb with a hammer – probably, I suspect, along with a few other rather less well-bred vocalizations. *Ouch* started life as the rather inadequate representation of the shriek or squeal we make when we're in pain, or rather what a German makes when in pain, since *ouch* is assumed to come from German. In fact *ouch* is nothing like the noise a German would make – the word has now totally assimilated to the English sound system.

Most of the more obvious German loans belong to the high-falutin level of our vocabulary: *Weltanschauung*, for instance, meaning 'world view'; *Schadenfreude* 'the pleasure you take in another's misfortune'; *Gestalt* 'pattern of experiences'. These still retain a fairly German-like pronunciation. Many also continue to be written with the capital letter characteristic of German nouns. If these words survive you can be sure they'll eventually assimilate. Look what's happened to *Angst*. It first entered English in the realm of psychoanalysis to describe a kind of neurotic anxiety or dread. It's now lost its capital letter, acquired a new English vowel sound and generalized its meaning – *angst* is used by many people for any kind of worry or fear.

Sometimes the assimilation process changes loan words beyond recognition. Even meanings can change significantly. The best example I know of is *hamburger*. This was originally an adjective derived from the placename Hamburg and referred specifically to meat from that area, just as *frankfurter* was originally meat from Frankfurt. In the case of *hamburger* the first part of the word happens to correspond to the English word *ham* and this encouraged speakers to reinterpret the word as a compound consisting of *ham* + *burger* (that hamburgers didn't actually involve ham didn't matter). English is a classic adapting language. Most of the words we purloin from other languages end up getting squashed into a kind of English mould. Look at *Kris Kringle* – it's come a mighty long way from dialectal German *Christkindl*, literally 'Christ child'.

But back to German *earworm*. Next time you have one of those irritatingly catchy little scraps of melody tootling about in your head you'll know what to call it. It's now official. It's an earworm.

25

My personal favourites

 When it comes to German loans I have a few personal favourites and it'll be interesting to see whether they ever make it into ordinary usage in the same way that *earworm* has. One I'm constantly using is *Schreibfaulheit* – literally 'writing laziness', but referring in particular to letter-writing. *I'm schreibfaul* means 'I'm a lousy letter-writer'. Another handy German word is *unbekannterweise*. There's no English word that comes anywhere near this one for convenience. Let me provide the context. Say you want to send your regards to someone you've never actually met. This you'd do *unbekannterweise*, which means you say hello without knowing the person – a handy word but unlikely to catch on, I suspect, because it's such a mouthful.

Another of my favourite German words, and one that *is* showing signs of catching on, is the verb *bummeln*. It's roughly equivalent to the English verb *to stroll*, and yet strolling doesn't convey quite the same idea of pleasantly frittering the time away. This sense of wandering idly is an important component of the meaning of *bummeln*. In fact, linguists suspect that *bummeln* is actually the source of that important English verb *to bum around* meaning 'to loaf about'. But *bummeln* is more picturesque and does, I reckon, deserve a place in Standard English. *To bummel* – it's a gorgeous word. (Mind you, as has been pointed out to me, Jerome K. Jerome's *Three Men on the Bummel* didn't manage to succeed in popularizing the word. But it's worth another try!)

All languages have expressions like *well, you know, I think, anyway*. These are always highly idiosyncratic and generally untranslatable. German has a particularly useful one – *doch*. Like all these features of talk, *doch* conveys a whole host of subtle nuances of meaning, but its most handy function is as a kind of affirmation. Someone might say to you, 'So you didn't like the meal', and you want to reply, 'No, on the contrary, I really enjoyed it'. In fact all you need say is *doch*. It says it all. English doesn't have anything quite this handy (although *yeah-no* comes close!). Languages never differ as to what they are able to express, but they do differ vastly as to what they express more easily.

Finally, I have another German expression that I would like to see make it into Standard English. I encountered it years ago when thumbing through a book of German idioms and I've been using it ever since. In fact, it's a loan translation. I've kept the idiom but rendered the German into English. The expression is *to play the injured liverwurst* meaning 'to be hurt or huffy'. This one must surely catch on – how could we do without it?

Dead horse and kate and sydney

While clearing out my library I chanced upon a collection of linguistic curiosities taken from Cockney slang. Among them was a range of wonderful rhyming slang terms for food, or what in rhyming slang might be called *tooting bec* (*bec* rhymes with 'peck' and presumably food is something you peck at). Here are some examples of this ingenious lingo: a Cockney *me and you* (in other words, a 'menu') might begin with *loop the loop* 'soup' or else *lillian gish* 'fish' followed by a nice bit of *kate and sydney* 'steak and kidney' or, if you'd prefer, some braised *down the drains* 'brains' – served of course with an assortment of *hasbeens* 'greens'. And for afters, highly recommended by the *babbler* (in other words the babbling brook or 'cook'), comes *smack in the eye* (or 'pie') and cream washed down with a fine selection of *string and twine* 'wine' and perhaps a platter of the best of English *stand at ease* 'cheese'.

Now, the surprising thing about this kind of slang is just how recent it is. There's really no sign of it before the 1800s. I couldn't find a single example in my copy of Captain Grose's *Dictionary of the Vulgar Tongue*, which dates from the 1780s. It's interesting that the later edition, from the 1850s, has around sixty-two rhyming slang entries. Most people assume these terms began life within criminal 'slanguage'. Certainly, this was where rhyming slang was first discovered, but this doesn't necessarily mean it originated there. Most likely it was the lexical invention of Cockney and Irish navvies and only later made its way into the cant of the Victorian underworld. But its criminal connections probably do account for the strong presence of rhyming slang in Australian English. Even though it doesn't figure nearly as much today as it once did, examples such as *kerry packered* 'knackered', *barossa pearl* 'girl', *germaine greer* 'beer' and *wally grout* 'shout' are clearly fairly recent and suggest the art of Australian rhyming slang has not completely died out.

In these last four examples the rhyme remains, but typically in rhyming slang today the expression has been shortened and the rhyming word gone. For example, *brahms* from *Brahms and Liszt* 'pissed, drunk', *khyber* from *Khyber Pass* 'arse', *rabbit (on)* from *rabbit and pork* 'to talk (incessantly)', *septic* from *septic tank* 'Yank'. The meanings of these clipped expressions derive from the unstated word which rhymes with the last part of the phrase. So when this word disappears, the sense is then transferred to the first part of the phrase and we have a meaning shift – sometimes quite a spectacular one. *Roast stop* for 'roast beef' only makes sense when you know it derives from the end-clipped phrase *Stop thief*, in other words 'beef' (originally the reference was to stolen beef).

Rhyming slang is of course a kind of verbal disguise, which is why it served the British underworld so well. It also provided linguistic fig leaves for many of the dirty words of the day. So effective was the disguise that a number have survived in our modern-day standard language, and are now used by speakers who for the most part are completely unaware of the underlying obscenity. While many of us use the expression 'He gets on my wick', few realise that this is in fact the clipped Cockney rhyming slang *Hampton wick*, in other words, 'prick'. Similarly, *cobblers!* from *cobbler's awls* stands for 'balls', *bottle* from *bottle and glass* for 'arse' and *I don't give a friar* from *Friar Tuck* – well, I'll leave you to supply the rhyme here. My mother would certainly describe a person as being 'a real berk', unaware that this derives from the longer expression *Berkeley hunt* (in turn rhyming slang for the body part one of my dictionaries coyly describes as 'the unprintable' and Captain Grose in his *Dictionary of the Vulgar Tongue* calls 'the monosyllable'). Many speakers still use the expression *to razz* someone meaning 'to tease, or make fun of them'. This is a shortened form of *raspberry*, the sound of contempt or derision, as in *to blow a raspberry*. This also began life as the end-clipped rhyming slang *raspberry tart*, in other words 'fart'. The same expression *raspberry tart* was also slang for 'heart' – but, as always happens, the vulgar has ended up dominating. Risqué senses never fail to kill off all the others!

Cocks' eggs

The word *cockney* itself has an interesting history. It goes back to late medieval English and derives from *cocken-ay*, literally 'cock's egg', an expression that was used initially for any small or mishapen egg (presumably an egg imagined to have been laid by a cock). German has the same expression – *Hahnenei*. The word *cockenay* then extended to refer to a pampered child or a 'milksop' (as such was once known) and from there to any sort of 'ineffective or useless fellow'. In the *Reeves Tale* Chaucer writes, 'When this jape is told another day, I sal be hald a daf, a cokenay'. In this sense it came to be applied contemptuously in the 1600s to a Londoner and eventually, in the 1800s, to the dialect or accent of the London Cockney.

As is typical of secret languages, Cockney rhyming slang serves a number of purposes. Certainly it's a verbal disguise that keeps all bystanders and eavesdroppers in the dark. But equally important is its social function – like slang generally, it defines the gang. And, of course, on top of all that it's a great deal of fun. This, I suspect, is the primary motivation for the use of Cockney rhyming slang today.

The cat's whiskers

The liveliness of the lexicon is very evident in our fondness for what can be thought of as vogue structures. For example, recently I was asked the origin of the curious phrase *the cat's whiskers*, as in *he's the cat's whiskers* – in other words, 'he's particularly good, or attractive'. Something that's *the cat's whiskers* is something remarkable, noteworthy, first rate. As is the case for so many of these kinds of expressions, the source here is mysterious. But what we do know about *the cat's whiskers* is that it is a remodelling of the earlier expression *the cat's pyjamas*. According to most lexicographers, this earlier expression appeared first in American English around 1920, then entered British English in the 1930s, and was alive and well until about 1940 when it was declared dead. Now, it might have been obsolete for American and British English, but both expressions were certainly current in Australian English when I was growing up. One dictionary editor, Paul Beale, acknowledges this. In his edition from 1984 of Partridge's celebrated *Dictionary of Slang and Unconventional English* he includes an endnote in the entries for both *the cat's whiskers* and *the cat's pyjamas*. It states 'far from dead in Australia'. Mind you, I'm not sure how lively these expressions are these days. I suspect they form part of the passive mental dictionary of many speakers but are not said very often, if at all. All of us have a vast resource of expressions that we may not use, but certainly recognise and understand – and *the cat's whiskers* and *the cat's pyjamas* are probably good examples.

But I'm straying from my point, which has to do with the energy and vitality of the lexicon. There are certain phrases that become so popular they encourage speakers to create similar expressions modelled on the same structure. The phrase becomes a formula and speakers bounce their creations off each other in a kind of language play. Wentworth and Flexner's *Dictionary of American Slang* describes *the cat's pyjamas* as one of the most popular fad expressions of the 1920s, and it appears to have spawned a whole heap of copy-cat constructions ('scuse the pun). In addition to *the cat's whiskers*, I've uncovered the *cat's miaow, the cat's eyebrows, the cat's ankle, tonsils, adenoids,* even *the cat's arse*. And there are various other cat trappings too, including *the cat's cufflinks, galoshes,* and *rollerskates*. All these are expressions once used to refer to something that was very, very good.

And then, around the 1930s, along came *the bee's knees*, also an expression for something attractive or noteworthy. Some lexicographers go into graphic detail about how bees – apparently – bend their knees in a very delicate fashion to carefully comb off the pollen in order to transfer it to the pollen sacs on their backs. Now, this may be the case, but my feeling is that it is not the likely motivation for this particular phrase. *The bee's knees* was surely coined on the pattern of *the cat's whiskers*, with the added catchiness of a rhyming pronunciation play. During the 1930s many similar expressions appeared. All combined animals with body parts or articles of clothing, sometimes to quite bizarre effect –

the eel's heel, the elephant's eyebrows or *instep, the gnat's eyebrows, the ant's eyebrows* are just a few of the creations I've come across.

Why our language changes is a fascinating question involving, as you'd imagine, a complex interaction of various social, psychological, linguistic and external (or language contact) forces at work. But even fashion is a factor. People want to change their language just as they change the hemlines on their trousers or dresses. Of course, in language there's probably not the deliberate manipulation you find in the fashion industry, but the same tug of war occurs between people's desire for new, exciting ways and the tendency of these ways to become routine and wear out. And this is most evident in vocabulary changes. Words, phrases and even affixes come in and out of fashion, and like modes of dressing they sometimes attain almost voguish popularity. For some reason, certain ones are taken up by a number of speakers and become buzz words. Suddenly they're everywhere. And like the lengths of hemlines and trouser legs, they're also usually short-lived – soon to be replaced by other buzz words. In some areas this generates a kind of semantic treadmill. When we buried *the cat's whiskers* there was no shortage of replacements. They included *far out* and *ace*. When these were no longer 'hip', they were supplanted by *cool* (this one has made something of a comeback). More recently we have seen *cool* fall by the wayside, pushed out by *wicked*. However, I gather no self-respecting teenager would be caught dead uttering *wicked* these days. The 'cool dudes' of the new millennium use the expression *phat* (or *fat*) for something that is 'outstanding' or 'first-rate' – I'd probably describe it as 'the bee's knees'.

The most irritating expressions

Early in 2004, the Plain English Campaign asked its five thousand supporters to nominate the phrases in the English language that most enraged them. Speakers in more than seventy countries were surveyed and the results were released in March. As it turned out, it was the expression *at the end of the day* that easily gained the most votes. In equal second place were *at this*

moment in time and the constant use of *like*. These were followed by the phrase *with all due respect*.

Overuse will always take the life out of an expression and there were plenty of 'lexical zombies' (to use David Crystal's label) on this list – *between a rock and a hard place, touch base, boggles the mind, bottom line, thinking outside the box, the fact of the matter is, moving the goalposts, pushing the envelope* and *singing from the same hymn sheet*. Others among the walking dead included intensifiers such as *absolutely* and *awesome*. These sorts of expressions always wear out quickly – and there's never a shortage of equally irritating replacements waiting in the wings. Presumably it's overuse, too, that puts *prioritize* on this list, although it might well be the *-ize/-ise* ending that gets up people's noses here – it has become something of a fad suffix of late. Sometimes suffixes and prefixes become so popular that they start to attract too much attention to themselves (and, of course, in this case you also have the '-ize' spelling – the final straw for many devotees or Fowler!).

Some expressions probably made the list because the Plain English supporters regarded them as misused. The word *epicentre*, for instance, gained a good number of votes. As I have mentioned earlier, this word is now frequently used in the general sense of simply 'middle'. It's a fairly new usage and has attracted a lot of bad press lately, most particularly from geologists. But a surprise appearance for me was *literally* – it's been 'misused' for so long I thought we'd all become immune. Certainly, in its core sense *literally* still means 'actually, not figuratively, without exaggeration'. However, when people say something like 'I was literally tearing my hair out', what they generally mean is that they were figuratively or metaphorically tearing out their hair – in other words, they weren't actually tearing out their hair at all! (*Literally* is virtually a contranym now – a word that is its own opposite.) Human beings are natural born exaggerators. We are constantly striving to enhance our expression and come up with new and exciting ways of saying things. It's this sort of extravagance that is behind the shift in meaning of both *literally* and *epicentre* – and typically, you'll find, the more recent the shift, the more annoying it is.

Of course, linguists like me who simply study language are not supposed to be irritated by this kind of usage at all. We aren't supposed to have linguistic hit lists, but find all expressions endearing. However, linguists are human too, and if you scratch the surface you'll usually uncover a little pile of pet hates. I was interested to see a number of mine on this list, including *bear with me, to be perfectly honest with you* and – one I particularly loath – *I hear what you're saying* . This last expression worries me greatly because when people say these words, it usually means they have absolutely no intention of attending to what I'm saying. Finally, there is one annoying Australianism I would place high on this list – the phrase *no worries*. The other day my phone rang at around 5.30 am. It turned out to be a wrong number. 'No worries!' chimed the caller cheerfully when I pointed this out. Surely, I'm not the only one irritated by this phrase?

Slang versus jargon

Not that long ago I received an interesting email from a person curious about the nature of slang, and in particular how it related to jargon. I at first thought this quite a straightforward question – but the longer I pondered on it the more tangled my response became.

Begin with slang. Now, people are always slinging off at slang. As someone early last century wrote, 'slang is to a people's language what an epidemic disease is to their bodily constitution'. Many connect it with swearing too, but this is in fact mistaken. Slang can be obscene, certainly, but it's not necessarily connected to taboo in the same way that swearing is. And as Lars Andersson and Peter Trudgill point out in their book on bad language, many people also wrongly identify slang with adolescent speech – as something we eventually grow out of. Certainly, teenagers use slang, but then so do adults. There are also those who view slang as a linguistic feature peculiar to modern times. This most certainly is not the case. Admittedly it's hard to make stylistic judgements on slang from the past, but slang has always been with us.

So what are the features that identify a piece of language as slang? For a start, it's obviously informal, usually spoken not written, and it involves mainly vocabulary rather than grammar. One striking feature is its playfulness. Metaphor, irony and sound association are important forces behind new slang expressions. Take colloquial terms for drunkenness like *sloshed, soused, smashed, sozzled, soaked, stewed* or even *steamed*. The (mostly liquidy) imagery here, you'll notice, is strongly underpinned by sound association. All these words begin with 's'. Another characteristic of slang is reduction of form. Teenagers from all around the English-speaking world use terms like *rents* (parents), *rad* (radical), and *dis* (disrespect).

But probably the most important feature of slang is that it's unstable. In fact, by the time this book appears in bookshops, *rents, rad* and *dis* will probably be well and truly passé. The whole point of slang is to startle, amuse, shock. It has to be short-lived. A study of university slang over a fifteen-year period showed that only 10 per cent of the expressions survived. If a slang expression does survive, then it's usually no longer slang. It's hard to imagine that such dull little words as *pants* and *mob* were once controversial slangy abbreviations.

Finally, slang serves the dual purpose of solidarity and secrecy. It indicates membership within a particular group, as well as social distance from the mainstream. At the same time, it prevents bystanders and eavesdroppers from understanding what's being said. This was in fact the original motivation of slang. When the word first appeared it referred specifically to the secret idiom of the British underworld.

And so, now to the second part of the query. How does slang differ from jargon? Like slang, poor old jargon is much maligned. Many people use the term pejoratively. Jargon is what turns 'a toothbrush' into 'a home plaque-removal implement' – it's intellectual hocus-pocus. When Keith Allan and I were investigating jargon in 1991 we came across the following glorious example from sociology – 'the objective self-identity as the behavioural and evaluative expectations which the person anticipates others having about himself'. Why doesn't the writer simply use the word *self-image*? (Of course, I could have taken an equally wonderful dollop of verbal flummery from my own discipline of linguistics – but it's always more fun to tilt at the jargon of others!) It's not surprising that *jargon* is frequently used contemptuously to describe language full of unfamiliar terms; in other words, 'articulate gibberish'.

But equally you could describe *jargon* as simply the language peculiar to a particular group of people such as a profession or a trade. To be fair, in the context of an article in the *British Journal of Sociology*, the gem of jargon I mentioned above doesn't look so bad – and presumably the writer didn't use it simply to augment his own objective self-identity as the behavioural and evaluative expectations which he anticipates others having about himself! Whether or not you apply the term *jargon* contemptuously will depend on whether you're a member of the group in question.

So jargon and slang do overlap. Both identify activities, events and objects that are routine for those involved. Both have an important function in creating rapport in the work or play environment. The difference is that slang is more colloquial and has a much faster turnover rate. Also, slang can usually be replaced by more standard expressions. Hence the dictionary description 'colourful, *alternative* vocabulary' [my emphasis here]. You could describe someone as *pickled*, *pissed* or *plastered*, or you could simply say they're *drunk*. It's true also that a lot of jargon is very replaceable. Legal language, for instance, is characterized by curiosities like *thereupon*, *hereinafter* and *herebefore*, which could easily be dispensed with, or at least replaced with modern-day equivalents. Like slang, jargon items such as these are a matter of style. They are built into the linguistic routine of this particular jargon and are now part and parcel of the rituals of the legal profession. But many jargon expressions don't have viable alternatives in ordinary language – the lawyer's *plaintiff*, the art historian's *skeuomorphy*, the linguist's *morpheme*, even the cricketer's *man at deep fine leg* and the footballer's *touch-down*. These refer to activities peculiar to each group and they fill a need. And in this respect, jargon can be very different from slang.

But there is one feature both slang and jargon always share – they have always been generous contributors to the ordinary English lexicon. Perhaps we should be more appreciative, for it's precisely sub-languages like these that maintain the fecundity of our fine English vocabulary.

Linguistic fig leaves

Line 5. Delete 'Bottlenecks', insert 'Localised Capacity Deficiencies'.

Amendment to a traffic plan for a London Borough, quoted in Cutts & Maher 1984, p. 45

A type of language that's closely meshed with slang and jargon is euphemism; in other words, expressions with more pleasing (or at least less offensive) associations than their alternatives. You could think of euphemism as a kind of linguistic dressing. It can be decorative, ornamental, flavour-enhancing, concealing – the kind of linguistic behaviour that turns *bottlenecks* and *traffic jams* into *localized capacity deficiencies.*

Certainly, there is much slang and jargon that automatically falls within the realm of euphemism. The setting and nature of the subject matter has significant bearing on this. Legalese is euphemistic when it deals with indecorous matters such as the *indecent exposure of the person* (where 'person' refers to 'penis'). In fact euphemism is arguably an essential part of the everyday running of the legal system. By convention, members of the legal profession are excessively polite to one another – everything is carried out *with (the greatest of) respect. In answer to my learned friend's erudite submission* is understood to mean 'you are wrong'. This is just one example of the sort of euphemistic doublespeak that goes on in a court room. Such masonic mortar allows you to sink the legal slipper (in other words, put the boot in) at the same time as maintaining an aura of goodwill and harmony.

A jargon such as Funeralese will always be dripping with euphemism, precisely because it deals with strong taboos on death. Funerals are usually *conducted* or *arranged* by *funeral directors* from *funeral parlours*, not any more by *morticians* or *undertakers* (these were earlier euphemisms). People involved in the business of collecting the body talk about *the removal* or *doing the contract.* We also come across startling slang expressions like *soup*, a term apparently used (privately) by some in the death industry to refer to 'a badly decomposing body' – a *floater* is one that has been fished out of water. This kind of gallows humour is euphemistic, in that it helps to lighten the grisly reality. Flippancy

36

towards what is feared is a way of coming to terms with that fear. And for those who have to deal with death and dying every day, the levity of slang expressions like this one makes the job easier to bear.

There are also euphemistic jargons, like those of politics and the military, that frequently add dimensions of guile and disguise. This is the sort of doublespeak that turns *death* into *a negative patient care outcome*, *dying* into *terminal living* and *killing* into *the unlawful deprivation of life*. Here lethal acts are cloaked in longwinded and technical expressions, presumably so that outsiders can't recognise them as easily and their impact is lessened. Perhaps it also suggests some shame on the part of the persons responsible – you'd like to think so. These are euphemisms loaded to the point of deception and, to my mind, they are probably the only really nasty weeds of the English language. More on them later in the book.

Closely related are sub-languages where jargon or slang are used as a kind of linguistic uplift or makeover. The 'official' language of poverty, for instance, is characterized by an abundance of euphemistic jargon like *indigent*, *impecunious* and *impoverished*. Poverty is an area of social taboo – an inevitable target for euphemism. This has led to a recent flourishing of dainty circumlocutions like *economically marginalized*, *negatively privileged*, *economically non-affluent*, or even *differently advantaged*. All are largely French or classically inspired. All tiptoe beautifully around the beastly business of poverty.

But what about the other, ordinary types of jargon and slang that fall well outside areas of social taboo? Take, for example, Cricketspeak. My colleague Keith Allan once revealed to me that in cricket 'a fast-medium right arm inswing bowler needs two or three slips, a deep third man, a gully, a deepish mid-off, a man at deep fine leg and another at wide mid-on'. Could this really be described as euphemism too? Presumably, an occupational jargon like Cricketspeak is the preferred lingo of people who play the game. It would therefore have pleasing connotations for those who are part of the cricket in-crowd. So in this sense it is a kind of euphemism, if on the outer bounds. Mind you, for those who aren't members of the club, terms such as *a deep third man* or *a deepish mid-off* can be befuddling, incomprehensible gobbledygook; in other words, dysphemism (the offensive counterpart to the sweet-smelling euphemism).

So yes, many uses of slang and jargon are indeed euphemistic. Both can be used to conceal fearful, and shameful, subjects. Both can sweeten the distasteful, even elevate the trivial. But all too often that same slang or jargon is, in the words of my Merriam–Webster's, 'confused unintelligible language'. If you're not part of the gang, euphemism quickly turns to dysphemism.

Linguistic flowers

 These days you don't come across much in the way of flowery, long-winded language of love. In the past these blooms were remarkably inventive and poetic – and often quite provocative. Writers have long been aware of the tingles provided by the artful use of euphemism. Look at that great poem 'The Romance of the Rose', a famous 13th-century allegory of the pursuit of the 'flower' of womanhood (where the rose stands as euphemism and symbol for the vagina). Early authors really knew how to exploit euphemism to portray a bawdy topic, while shielding themselves from any shocked reader's protests by establishing the defence that – well, the text is wholly innocent. Any risqué interpretation is merely a construction of the reader's mind. For instance – if you think 'The Romance of the Rose' is a text about the pursuit of pudendum, and not the quest of some lover to pluck a rose from an enchanted garden, then that's just your grubby little imagination. The entire romance is, of course, a literary lie. Not that medieval audiences were necessarily known for their prudishness – but one of the reasons these texts are successful is that they exploit euphemism to publicly expound taboo topics, while at the same time pretending to disguise that purpose. And like any tease, such a disguise may itself be titillating.

Look at Shakespeare – the all-time master of the euphemistic bawdy. As linguists like Eric Partridge and, more recently, Keith Allan have shown, in Shakespeare's low comedy sexual innuendo works through euphemistic metaphors. Shakespeare is successful exactly because this veiled eroticism achieves a heightened reality. Or think of those writing during the early Victorian period. Once again, these writers were remarkable for their ability to produce sexual humour without ever using a single sex word. Again we see euphemism at work to shield the writer against accusations of being offensive, while at the same time teasing the mind with double-meanings. The wedding night of Queen Victoria, for instance, has been described variously as a kind of military advance, an exploratory foray, or a simple essay in horse-riding. And, of course, once within the safe haven of whatever analogy the writer chooses, there is no holding back – the story achieves the heightened reality endowed by an effective double-entendre and conceals just enough to become all the more prurient and alluring. These authors were brilliant at it.

Vague, flowery, circumlocutory language of love is not always as coy and innocent as it pretends. Like diaphanous garments, these linguistic wraps are often not intended as camouflage. These are provocative euphemisms.

Partners and paramours

The term *partner* has been around for some time now to describe one member of a couple. They might be married or live together or perhaps are lovers. For some reason this word *partner* remains a source of considerable irritation to a good many people. Perhaps it's the bland nature of the expression. It also brings to mind business associates, colleagues, dancing companions or even players who are on the same side in a game. But it is a handy term, you'll have to admit. Labels such as *husband*, *wife*, *de facto*, *spouse* and so on only include those relationships sanctioned by a legal or quasi-legal union. A term such as *partner* nicely sidesteps that issue, and is therefore more representative. Besides, what's the alternative? A *live-in lover* sounds more like a lodger or a boarder – almost certainly the stay is short-term. *Significant other* was popular for a while but never really took off. I suppose we could always create a new acronym – *spipc* or 'sexual partner in permanent cohabitation'. After all, American English has already given us the *posslq* 'person of opposite sex sharing living quarters'. Personally I'd prefer it if we brought back something like *paramour*. You can always rely on the French language to supply some piquancy – and the fact that the expression once referred to 'an illicit lover' gives it just that little bit more *je ne sais quoi*.

Of course, for years French has been supplying English with expressions involving intimacy, particularly if it's of an 'irregular' nature. *Beau* and *gallant* have probably bitten the dust, as have *assignation* and *tryst*, but we still use *affair*. This use dates from the early 18th century. Somewhat later the word acquired a final 'e'. Its French appearance made it all the more erotic. *Affaire* arrived sometime during the 19th century, as did *liaison*. Now, I've always felt there to be something rather delicious about the French word *liaison*. Perhaps it's the fact that it derives from a cooking term that referred originally to the 'thickening of sauces' – one recipe from the 1750s, for instance, instructs how to 'prepare a liaison, of four or five yolks of eggs and some cream'. From this meaning it shifts easily to the more general sense of 'intimate association or relationship' and from there slips beautifully into its current meaning of 'illicit sexual association'. (As an aside, notice how we use even the adjective 'French' – *French vice*, 'sexual malpractices'; *French prints*, 'pornographic pictures'; *French kiss*, 'a deep kiss'; *French disease/French pox*, 'venereal disease'; *French letter/French tickler*, 'condom' – *French* has, as my dictionary puts it, 'the implication of spiciness'!)

By comparison our common current-day expressions, especially the English-based ones, appear to have no sexual connotations at all. What have we got but unimaginative understatements such as *friend* (and its various compounds such as *boyfriend, girlfriend, gentleman friend, lady friend*), or *companion* (especially the *constant companion*). Two people romantically inclined are even described as *an item*. Not much in the way of linguistic titillation there! Then there are the expressions such as *to go out with*, or *take out*, or *see* someone. 'One's regular sexual partner' becomes *this guy/girl I've been seeing*. Nowadays you'd think we're all pretty up-front about love. Nonetheless, the coy nature of these various vague expressions suggests we're still a little blushful about sexual encounters, at least when they touch us personally.

What ever happened to the belly?

Some time back I had an interesting email enquiry regarding the word *belly*. Why – this person wanted to know – do we use the word *stomach* for this part of the body, when really the stomach refers to the internal organ contained within the belly? She's right. *Belly* has virtually disappeared from ordinary usage and *stomach* has taken its place, shifting its reference to include that part of the body roughly between the diaphragm and the groin, as well as the organ of digestion contained within it. *Belly* is really only used these days in a handful of compound expressions like *belly-dancing*, *belly-up* and occasionally *belly laugh*. In a sense, the word *belly* is going the same way as early English *hriff*, an expression that once referred to precisely the same body part as *belly*. *Hriff* has now virtually disappeared from English, lingering on only in the little relic that remains in the expression *midriff*.

It was really during the Victorian era that *belly* fell from grace. This was the time when people were particularly queasy about any body part anywhere near the belt or below it. Recall the terms used in novels of this time, invisible words such as *inexpressibles, unmentionables, indescribables, ineffables, inexplicables, unspeakables, unutterables* and so on – all to avoid saying those shameful words for the garments that covered the (unmentionable) legs. Small wonder the *belly* was in trouble. In the public arena it was expunged from texts. For example, when in the 1830s Noah Webster set about cleaning up the Bible he replaced expressions such as *in the belly* with *in the embryo*. It was also during this time that *stomach* started to appear in place of *belly*. *Belly-ache* became *stomach-ache* – apparently even Aubrey Beardsley's illustration in the first edition of Wilde's *Salome* in 1894 was entitled *Stomach Dance*.

Vagueness, of course, is what you want in a euphemism, and many euphemistic substitutions involve expressions that refer indirectly to something risqué. The most successful euphemisms are those where this association lacks any sort of precision. The vaguer the better. Even the word *viscera* transformed itself by euphemistic magic from the interior organs like the stomach, intestines, lungs and heart into that surface part of the body between the diaphragm and the groin – in other words, 'the belly'. Expressions like *stomach* and *viscera* are safe body parts located somewhere nearby the bawdy part. But then what usually happens is that the next generation of speakers grows up learning the euphemism as the direct term for the shameful thing – and brand new euphemisms must be found. Peter Fryer in his *Studies of English Prudery* provides ample evidence that during the late 1800s people were beginning to feel a tad queasy about *stomach* as well. Apparently, Trollope allowed his publisher to change the phrase *fat stomach* to *deep chest* in *Barchester Towers*. Human anatomy clearly is of no consequence when euphemism is at work, and body part terms become very slippery indeed!

But let me not give the impression that everything to do with risqué body parts was deadly serious. People also clearly had fun dreaming up appropriate linguistic fig leaves. There was a lot of verbal play. The belly became *the bread-basket, the pudding house, the middle pie*. During this period the remodellings *tum* and *tummy* appeared. *Stomach-ache* occasionally became *a pain in one's pinny*, with *pinny* a shortened form of *pinafore* – not even a body part, and so a double disguise for the dreadful belly.

The trepidation surrounding bellies lingered even into the 20th century. Alec Craig in his book *Sex and Revolution*, published in 1934, tells a story from his childhood. Apparently, Alec was at a party where children were playing a game that involved adding a *-y* ending to their names to derive diminutive forms like *Jamesy, Alfy* and so on. One little girl was called *Belle* and so, of course, there was a terrible hullabaloo when a child spoke the unspeakable by adding the suffix – *belly* was *still* not a word to be spoken out loud, particularly by the young and the innocent.

These days you'd imagine we've all become fairly laid-back about the belly. No need for any sort of comical camouflage. But this is not entirely true. The belly remains problematic when it happens to be particularly ample, and here's where you find euphemism today. Foreign terms can be relied upon for putting a good spin on 'big-belliedness' – *ventripotent*, for instance, from the Latin, or *embonpoint* from the French. Fat bellies have become *bagels, bay windows, love handles, rubber tyres* or *spare tyres*. And for the beer belly, you can always rely on Australian English for a colourful euphemism – one of my favourites is the *big verandah above the toy shop*.

Where do body parts come from?

The belly question got me thinking generally about the origins of our body part terms. *Belly*, it turns out, is the same word historically as *bellows* (this is the plural form) and both go back to a word which in Old English meant something like '(cloth) bag' or 'shell' (as of a pea). This is very typical. When we are lucky enough to be able to uncover the source concepts of body terms, what we often find are common vocabulary items that have been extended to provide new terminology.

For example, the Latin word for 'pot' *testa* provides the source for the current French word for 'head' *tête* – the Latin 'pot' may also give us our word *testicle.* Usually these everyday items show some sort of similarity in shape and function that makes them an obvious model, particularly when it comes to naming less conspicuous body parts. Linguist Bernd Heine, who has looked closely at the topic of bodies and language, gives some lovely illustrations. Small mammals such as mice and rats often serve as structural templates for 'muscle', or indeed muscular parts of the body like thigh, calf and biceps. Our word *muscle* is an example. It derives from the Latin word *musculus* meaning 'little mouse'. Some languages recruit other small animals for their body part terms, such as lizards, rabbits and toads. Usually the visual imagery is obvious. I mentioned the word *testicle* earlier. In many languages the source concepts here are items such as eggs, stones, pebbles, seeds and fruits. In English, of course, we have plenty of colloquial examples – testicles as *balls, nuts, acorns, stones* and *rocks* (as in *get one's rocks off*).

Whether we're producing names for new concepts or simply adding to the names of old ones, metaphor is often behind it all. We are always adapting familiar structures from our experiences to new purposes and our body part terminology supplies wonderful illustrations of this. Many of the figures we create are very inventive and there's a lot of verbal play involved. I think my favourite example is still *the miraculous pitcher, that holds water with the mouth downwards.* This extraordinary example comes from the 18th century – it was a euphemism for 'vagina'. (But then again, Australian English *budgie smugglers* for a 'tight pair of men's swimming trunks' would come a close second!)

Body parts behaving badly

Body part terms themselves, such as blood, ear, eye, hand/arm, head, heart, leg/foot, mouth, stomach, tongue and tooth, often end up naming less basic body parts.

Linguists have observed that languages typically behave the same way in these transfers. For example, Bernd Heine describes something he dubs the 'top-down strategy'. Such a transfer of patterns between different parts proceeds from the UPPER to the LOWER body; for instance, toes are often referred to as 'fingers of the foot', but fingers will never be called the 'toes of the hand'. In many languages the anklebone is the 'eye of the foot', but eyes are never 'anklebones of the head'. The terms for 'neck' or 'wrist' often extend to include the 'ankle', but never the other way around. The reason for this is probably because the upper half of the body is perceptually more salient than the lower half. So you may find the nipple being described as the 'nose of breast' and the knee the 'head of leg'. Only occasionally do you find exceptions, where lower body part terms are extended to upper body parts. One African language, for instance, describes the elbow as the 'knee of the arm'. But this sort of thing is very rare, and where it does occur it is always front body parts (like knee) transferring to those parts at the back of the body (like elbow), again probably because the parts located at the front are the more obviously visible ones.

Frequently, speakers will recruit body part terms from other body parts that are close by. Linguists such as David Wilkins and Bernd Heine have observed that this is a uni-directional transfer from small to large, or part to whole – for example, the extension of belly or navel to body, hand to arm, foot to leg and so on. English *belly* provides an example of this. For a short time very early on in its history *belly* was used generally to describe the entire human body. In this case, though, the use wasn't long-term.

This part-for-whole strategy is very common for ordinary body parts. Let me emphasize, however, that it doesn't hold for those we'd rather not talk about. Here you'll find it's the opposite strategy at work – the whole always comes to name the part. The legal term *person* for 'penis' (as in the *indecent exposure of the person*) is a superb example. *Chest* for 'female breast' provides another. This, of course, is driven by euphemism. A speaker who wants to refer to the anatomical 'below the belt' parts can resort to vague and very general 'geographical' words such as *groin, loin* and *nether regions.* These shift the focus to the general area where these unmentionable bits are roughly situated. *Groin,* for instance, originally referred to the area where the thigh meets the body. Its location made it a kind of all-purpose euphemism for anything unmentionable in that general region. The *loins* were the bit below the ribs and above the hips, so once again it's the general-for-the-specific-body-part-located-somewhere-close-by strategy!

You will find that if the opposite strategy – part-for-whole – is employed, the effect is usually offensive. For example, *chest* is obviously a euphemism when used for female breasts, but *tits* 'nipples' is definitely not. You could also compare the extension of body part terms such as *prick* or *arsehole* as insults – for instance, the epithet *he's a prick.* (By the way, this figurative use of body parts as terms of abuse is a feature of Modern English swearing and is a fairly recent phenomenon in English – early last century, in fact, for *prick.*)

Bawdy body parts always behave linguistically very differently from other body parts. You'd expect this – after all, they're taboo. But in one respect they definitely do not differ. When speakers enlist new expressions for body part terminology, bawdy or otherwise, very little regard is ever shown for the finer points of human anatomy. Ordinary language can take body part terms a mighty long way from their medical specifications.

Rattling naughty – is it really English?

A friend of mine purchased a new microphone not that long ago. It was a very fine microphone, too, and from a very reputable overseas manufacturer. However, what was most remarkable

More body parts

The significance of the body in shaping patterns of language-use also shows up in the way we employ body part terms to describe other ordinary vocabulary items. English, for instance, provides many examples where words like mouth, foot, neck and eye have extended to inanimate objects like rivers, mountains, bottles and potatoes. We talk about *the leg of the table, the tongue of the shoe, the bowels of the building* and so on. Usually there is some kind of relationship between the body part and the item it comes to describe, for instance, an association to do with shape, size, function or perhaps even the location of the part relative to other body parts. We might call the prominent or projecting part of objects a 'nose'; think of bows on ships or muzzles on guns. Interestingly, the same few body parts seem to get exploited in this way – generally, it's our most conspicuous ones.

about this particular microphone was the description that appeared on the accompanying box. Now, I have encountered many strange examples of English, particularly on packaging, but this would have to be one of the most curious. Here is how the features of the microphone were described. (And no, the punctuation and capitals are not typos.)

We have got the world divided into boxes. each box is a science, and inside it we have locked. From the vast maternal quarry. Nature, And so, in little heaps assembled by chance or perhaps.

It sounds rather beautiful but I have absolutely no idea what any of it means. I've never thought of microphones as being particularly poetic things but this description does have a kind of dream-like quality to it. Certainly the grammar is imaginative. And the punctuation shows a very decorative application of commas and a delightfully creative use of full-stops and random capital letters.

Food packaging is also always a source of unusual English. I'm very grateful to Amy Williams for passing on to me her empty noodle packet. The 'Choiceness Grocery Nation Affirmation' on the back is a lovely read:

'We are the first company of our country to obtain the GMP & ISO 9002 of the dried noodles. It is non-fried and never adding any preservatives. The quality is health and satisfaction. You can set your mind at ease, because we can safeguard your expenditure.'

I'm also indebted to Santa for putting four magic laundry balls in my Christmas stocking. According to the instructions, these balls work by 'turning with laundries, prevent to twisting of each laundries and striking the dirty parts on laundries'. Apparently this makes for 'great efficient washing'.

One of my favourites is still the English that appears on the back of a French tin of snails. I owe Rita Erlich for this gem – Rita got the tin of snails from her friend John Cashmere who had brought it back from France. So no, I didn't make it up. The instructions on the tin begin: 'To hold one box, open at cooling'. Now that's instructive. And then come directions for the preparation of what is aptly described on the tin as the 'farce'. (Presumably some kind of stuffing. It's difficult to know how to make it from the description – but in case you should wish to try, it requires around one dozen snails.) And this is what you do:

'With 5 g of parsley, to join 4 g of garlic, 1 g of shallot, 4 g of salt, one prim of pepper, the half of one nut. To hew him and to mix at 50g of butter very fine. To drain the put in the shells, to furnish of farce claseborder, to passt at over hot one quarter time about'.

So, is this all part of some cunning plan hatched by the French Academy to get their own back on English, I wonder?

The global spread of English beyond the secure confines of its mother-tongue countries has certainly meant some extraordinary adjustments for the language and its speakers. What is clear is that a singular designation of English is today quite inadequate to describe a language that now involves almost every linguistic area in the world. So English has a radical new plural form – *Englishes*.

Indeed, we need a range of new labels like *Modern Englishes, World Englishes, New Englishes* and *Other Englishes* to cover the important varieties that have sprung up as a consequence of this global expansion.

We probably also need a range of blended labels too, such as *Japlish, Spanglish, Frenglish* and *Anglikaans*, for the varieties of English that appear on microphone boxes and tasty noodle packets. However, I'm not sure how you'd classify these written curiosities of what could be thought of as global advertising-speak. The world over, you find items of clothing such as T-shirts, jackets and jeans (and indeed, everything from rubbers – or erasers if you prefer – to shopping bags) all sporting curious English slogans. A colleague of mine has a T-shirt with the extraordinary slogan 'Rattling Naughty. I have an itch to play skateboard'. So why use English here? Well, the reason is simple. English sells. It has to do with the practicalities of a global *lingua franca* to be sure, but probably even more it has to do with power – cultural power, and above all economic power. Simply putting an English message on a product can make it somehow more appealing or more exciting to a non-English speaker – it doesn't even have to make sense.

But let's not be smug here. The correct use of foreign languages has never been of concern to English speakers when it comes to advertising. Look at what we do to French, especially in the language of food: *Stuffed Tomato aux Herbes, Shoreham Style; Le Crab Meat d'Alaska au Sherry, Flaming Coffee Diablo, Prepared en Vue of Guest* – well, there's a mixture! The Romance languages like French and Italian connote culinary excellence for speakers of English. French, of course, is especially sexy. It speaks to us of sophistication, elegance – and, like the English on T-shirts and shopping bags, it's what sounds good that's important. None of it has to make sense – unless of course you did want to understand the instructions on the article you've just bought, and then you're in trouble.

More Lexical Weeds:
Word Origins and Meaning Shifts

The Chickweed grows everywhere on rich cultivated land. Now we find it springing up in the garden, after a spring rain, making the beds green with its young shoots, and even in winter having the light tint of the spring leaf. In the fields it calls for the weeder's care; and under the hedge bank its white flowers bloom all the year long, save when the snows have covered every green thing. It is a very valuable plant to birds; nor is it one of the worst of those herbs which men have sometimes boiled for their food. We need hardly describe its small flower, for it may always be seen, like a little star among its leaves, when the sun is shining.
Anne Pratt *The Flowering Plants, Grasses, Sedges and Ferns of Great Britain* 1889

Popular etymologies

Etymology is the study of the origin and history of words. It's a subject that fascinates most people – and it's often full of surprises. For example, dictionary makers and dictionary users can have quite different ideas about how a certain word or expression has come into being. Most of us have stories about the history of some word or other, and we're shocked (often irritated) when we find no mention of these in the dictionary. Lexicographers do sometimes spoil our fun with their cautious labels: 'of uncertain origin' or 'etymology unknown'. But you can't blame them. Unfortunately, there's usually no evidence for these marvellous linguistic tales. Worse than that, the chronology is often completely wrong. In this case, they are almost certainly spurious.

Let me go through a few of the most popular and persistent of these stories. Many, you'll find, involve acronyms, that is, words formed from the initial letters of other words. For instance, some people have it that Australian English *wowser*, meaning 'prude, killjoy', derives from the phrase '**w**e **o**nly **w**ant **s**ocial **e**vils **r**emedied', but this is most certainly a clever linguistic invention after the fact. You have to be careful with acronyms – some make good stories, but they may not always reflect the true origin of the word. The etymology of *wowser* remains obscure (although it is possibly connected with a British dialect word *wow* 'to whine, whinge').

Posh is another well-known example. The story goes like this – you've probably heard it many times already – on voyages between Britain and India, cabins on the side away from the sun were the most desirable and of course the most expensive. On the way out this was 'port side' and on the way home, 'starboard side'. The well-heeled travellers, therefore, went 'port out, starboard home' and the initials P-O-S-H were supposedly written on documents and luggage to indicate this. *Posh* then came to mean 'elegant, first-class'. Good story, but there are problems. One of the research team associated with *The Oxford English Dictionary* made a thorough investigation of shipping documents. According to dictionary editors Jeremy Marshall and Fred McDonald, he even consulted regular travellers, but without uncovering a shred of evidence to support this tale. In addition, the dates don't mesh. *Posh* was around in the early 1900s. This story didn't start circulating until some twenty years later. So once more it's 'etymology unknown', I'm afraid.

The expression *OK* (or *okay*) is one that has spawned an extraordinary array of bogus etymologies based on languages from all over the world. West African, Greek, American Indian and French origins have been proposed – even Scots *och aye* has been suggested as a likely source. One of the most imaginative stories derives it from the boxing term *KO* (or *kayo*), an abbreviation for 'knock out'. If the boxer wasn't kayoed, then he was *OK*! Nice – but no! *KO* appeared more than eighty years after *OK*. The story that's best supported by documentary evidence and wins the approval of the dictionary makers is in fact one that bases it on an acronym. *OK* derives from a jokey misspelling around in the 1830s of the expression *all correct* – 'orl korrekt'. (There was also *OW* for 'oll wright'.) According to *The Oxford English Dictionary* editors, what helped to popularize *OK* was the fact that it was adopted as an election slogan by supporters of the Democratic candidate Martin Van Buren. He was born in Kinderhook (New York State) and this earned him the nickname Old Kinderhook. His supporters then formed the Old Kinderhook Club or the OK Club in order to solicit money for campaigns. The term really took off in the 20th century and has now become a truly international word.

The expression *OK* tells us something interesting about the histories of popular expressions. Some time back when a colleague Keith Allan and I were exploring the ins and outs of slang, what struck us was just how many of our more prolific slang terms have mongrel origins; in other words, a number of influences coming together to help establish the meaning of the form – just as with *OK*. It almost seems that for an expression to be successful it needs this sort of reinforcement. So even if many of the tales surrounding our favourite words are phony, if the story of their origin captures our imagination in this way, the expressions probably have a much better chance of becoming established and surviving.

The real etymology of nylon?

 The origin of the word *nylon* is something of a linguistic mystery. One popular etymology bases it on a kind of acronym, a blending of the placenames New York and London. This is most definitely not the case. Most wordsmiths in fact claim the word *nylon* is etymologyless. Robert Stockwell and Donka Minkova in their book on English words describe it as rare example of a true coinage; in other words, an arbitrary arrangement of letters that is not based on any pre-existing word or part of a word. It is said to have been coined by the Du Pont Company when they first developed the material. Mind you, there would have been pre-existing words, such as *electron*, that could have provided the model, so product names like *Nylon* and also *Orlon, Dacron* and *Teflon* are not perhaps completely out of the blue.

American linguists Thomas Pyles and John Algeo point out, however, that Du Pont's own records suggest something quite different. When the material was first developed, it was given the extraordinary name *polyhexamethyleneadipamide* – not likely to catch on as a trade name! Apparently, the company did toy with the idea of calling it *duprooh*, a cunning acronym for 'Du Pont pulls rabbit out of hat', but ended up settling for *no-run*. Unfortunately for Du Pont, the stockings turned out not to be run-proof. So they reversed the spelling of *norun* and got *nuron*. The word was then changed to *nilon*, as Pyles and Algeo suggest, to make it sound less like a nerve tonic. Later the spelling was altered so people wouldn't pronounce it 'nillon'. If this is all true, then this time the real etymology is more exciting than the popular one – *nylon* isn't a boring old acronym after all.

Getting down to the nitty-gritty

During the 1990s, just about wherever you looked you came upon newspaper articles about political correctness: 'Cliché of the decade', 'University Faces Struggle in Political Correctness Debate', 'It's a Sexist, Racist, Fatist, Ageist World', 'Will Political Correctness Kill Free Speech Here Too?', 'Gay and Jew Get New Deaf Signs in NZ'. And remember all those anecdotes about the *differently hirsute*, *the specially non-tall* and the *chronologically gifted*? I was under the impression that the fuss had all died down, but I was wrong. A spate of news stories in the last few years suggests that the PC controversy is as hot as it ever was. Let me recount an instance reported in the London *Daily Telegraph*.

Apparently, in May 2002 a British government minister was severely criticised for his use of the phrase *nitty-gritty* at a police conference, because of its supposed racist overtones. He evidently had told his audience that it was high time to 'get down to the nitty-gritty' in training officers. It seems that in the modern British police service the expression *nitty-gritty* is prohibited because it's thought to have originally referred to those in the lowest reaches of slave ships. This etymology is spurious. I can find nothing to link the word to the early slave trade. It appears, in fact, to have entered English quite recently – sometime during the 1960s, probably via Black English and initially as a bit of popular music slang.

It would seem that the London police force has quite a list of 'dirty' words. These include the expressions *egg and spoon* and *a good egg*. The police are correct with their history of *egg and spoon*. Along with *harvest moon* and *silvery spoon* the term was originally 19th-century Cockney rhyming slang for 'coon'. Its use has always been racist. Now, although there's nothing to link it historically with other *egg* expressions, such is the power of taboo that a blameless bystander like *a good egg* 'a good chap' (as opposed to *a bad egg* 'a disreputable person') is automatically affected and itself tabooed.

Another expression on the police 'hit list' is *pikey*. This is a close relative to that beloved piece of Aussie lingo *piker* and its verb form *to pike out* 'to opt out'. *Pikey* was an 18th-century slang term (originally from *turnpike*), used in reference to vagabonds and beggars. It's not clear why *pikey* has fallen from grace in British English. Perhaps it's the phonetic similarity with the racially offensive word *ikey*. Or perhaps it is felt to be offensive to street people, in which case, if you ban *pikey* (and by association also Australian English *piker*) you should most certainly also ban *rogue*, *rascal* and *ratbag*, not to mention those other 'shocking' words *scoundrel* and *scallywag*. These were all once highly contemptuous terms for vagrants and vagabonds but, as is often the case, exaggerated use has caused them to shed their appalling connotations. All of these words have now virtually lost their wounding capacity.

Here, of course, lurks a real problem with this whole business of legislating against 'words that wound'. Language is not a perfect linguistic system but full of indeterminacy, variability and ambiguity. Any linguistic legislation will always have to be vague enough to allow for contextual differences and this makes it virtually unenforcable. The words *rogue*, *rascal*, *ratbag*, *scoundrel* and *scallywag* are now quite playful, in some contexts almost terms of endearment. Most Australians would argue that the word *piker* is also usually used in a jocular, even affectionate, fashion. The choice between alternative expressions will always depend on context. Word meanings and their associations vary continuously in response to different situational factors. Quite simply, offensiveness is never an intrinsic quality of a word, but rather of the way it is used. And for that reason it makes no sense whatsoever just to outlaw a word.

Many of the examples on the police list involve popular etymologies that have little basis in linguistic fact. Normally they're a bit of fun, but in the PC arena they can be used much like creedal cudgels. Even if the etymologies were correct, they should never be employed as a justification for banning. The belief that a word's origin dictates what it really means is a piece of fuzzy thinking, especially when it's used to support a particular point of view. It was once claimed, for instance, that men couldn't be hysterical. Since *hysteria* comes from the Greek word for 'womb', male hysteria was a contradiction. If using etymology this way were valid, then the course I give on English grammar should include instruction in magic, since the word *grammar* goes back to an earlier meaning of 'magical lore' or 'the study of the incomprehensible' (which perhaps still holds true for some students!). And, of course, in the area of political correctness and linguistic taboo, when you argue in this way you open the flood gates for the banning of a whole host of innocent words for their supposed offensive origins. Do we therefore ban all *egg* expressions? OK, granted *egghead* can be offensive to bald people – and also to academics – but what about the *curate's egg*, *egg on one's face*, and *teaching your grandmother to suck eggs*? Should these go too?

I recognise the problem with my argument here. Sound linguistic reasoning is not always protection for an innocent expression. As is so often the case, it doesn't really matter what linguistic science suggests, but how speakers perceive their language to be. If people do start connecting *nitty-gritty* with the N-word, *pikey* with *ikey* and *a good egg* with *egg and spoon*, then this will be the kiss of death for these expressions. *Fuk* 'a sail' and *feck* 'efficiency' had absolutely nothing to do with the dreaded F-word either, but that didn't save them.

'Niggerdly'

 Many readers will recall the controversy sparked off in 1999 by the use of the word *niggardly* by David Howard, an employee in the Washington DC mayoral office. Howard evidently had told his staff that in light of cutbacks he would have to be 'niggardly' with funds. Many connected this word with the highly tabooed word *nigger* and the uproar that followed resulted in his resignation.

In the Internet posting 'American political correctness and the word "niggardly"', Anders Jacobsen describes another more recent incident. In September 2002 Stephanie Bell, a fourth-grade teacher at Williams Elementary School (Wilmington, USA), taught the word *niggardly* to her students – and apparently, at least one parent wanted her fired. Links to Jacobsen's discussion mention a number of similar events.

The reactions to Anders Jacobsen's 'niggardly' posting were interesting. Mike Pugh's response, for example, was typical. 'I've always had a problem with the term "niggardly". It's always been my least favorite word in the English language. Yes, it's not technically racial slang, but I do think that people with cultural sensitivity and taste avoid using the term.' In another reply, George from CARM describes how he also shuns the terms *reneger* and *reneged* – 'I have noticed myself using a different way to convey my message when I am around black people', he wrote. The problem, it seems, is that second syllable in the verb *renege* 'deny, renounce' is pronounced in his variety of English as '–nig'.

Clearly, the reality that *niggardly* and *reneger* have absolutely no etymological connections with *nigger* is of no consequence here. Speakers will always sidestep expressions that remind them of taboo words. *Regina* makes some people feel uncomfortable beause of its phonetic similarity to *vagina* and they avoid it. *Cunny* (or *coney*) 'rabbit' dropped from the lexicon when it took on, as one lexicographer delicately put it, 'inappropriate anatomical significance'. Gender, sexuality, disability and especially race terms are now so highly-charged that speakers will shun anything that may be interpreted as discriminatory or pejorative – and this includes any innocent bystanders that just happen to get in the way.

Political correctness – iron hand of coercion or velvet glove of consensus?

Linguistic legislation generally has a lousy track record when it comes to getting people to 'reform' their linguistic behaviour. Typically we do our own thing regardless of what the authorities tell us. In this respect, the phenomenon called political correctness has been interesting. Whatever you may think of it, political correctness has been remarkably effective in getting people to alter their language habits, far more effective than other kinds of prescriptive practices. The so-called generic *he* (as in *if a student wants to, he can collect the reading lists at the office*) and terms such as *chairman, man-made, lady doctor, woman priest* and *authoress* are rarely encountered these days.

People generally don't like linguistic change, especially when it smacks of deliberate manipulation. And the success is all the more remarkable here, given that political correctness is not a movement that anyone appears to endorse. People whinge about losing what they see as their freedom to 'call things by their right names', as it's sometimes put, and complain endlessly about the need to rescue words that have been hijacked by it. Moreover, PC-motivated name changes are seen by many as 'the thin end of the wedge' that will work to fragment society into different factions and special interest groups. All this hostility is further fuelled by media hyperbole and misrepresentation.

So how do we explain the success of political correctness in changing people's linguistic behaviour? Certainly there have been some legal restrictions imposed on open expression. In the USA, for example, there have been formal speech codes imposed on certain campuses and other kinds of official prohibitions that make it an offence to use expressions deemed sexist, racist, homophobic or anti-Semitic. In some celebrated instances people have even been packed off to sensitivity workshops. But this sort of restraint and repression is by no means commonplace and restrictions are always difficult to enforce. Perhaps, then, the linguistic changes we're seeing result from the many manuals of non-discriminatory language that have been published over the years. But I'm not convinced that language change is ever a direct consequence of the recommendations of handbooks and style guides. These linguistics authorities are only ever guidelines – in the end they rely on people making their own personal decisions to alter their language. Perhaps the changes we're seeing are simply the inevitable outcome of, say, successful equal-opportunity practices; in other words, a natural linguistic evolution in the face of more general social change. Certainly, language change typically follows social change, rather than the other way around.

But I also think what's going on here is the voluntary censoring of speech. Glenn Loury, writing on political correctness in the 1990s, claimed at that time that political correctness had created a climate of tacit censorship. A violation of PC protocol, he argued, could quickly turn into an enquiry into a person's character. And he's right; when people express themselves in an 'incorrect' way, there's a danger their audience will judge them by others who have spoken in a similar way, and this can mean true racists, true homophobes, true misogynists – bigots whose motives *are* malevolent. People are always mindful of what expressions might 'sound' like, and they won't take risks – and so the safest thing is to adopt the PC-approved terminology.

What we're seeing isn't really so very different from what occurs in other taboo areas, whether these involve bodily functions, sex, death, disease or whatever. It has to do with the striking nature of tabooed terms. Derogatory or unfavourable meanings and associations always dominate the interpretation of expressions, and speakers will simply not risk appearing to use a 'dirty word' when none was intended. In the 19th century those in polite society were so fearful of impropriety that they avoided the terms *leg* and *breast*, even when speaking of a cooked fowl. They referred instead to *dark meat* and *white meat*. In a failure to follow a PC regime there's more at stake. Just look at those flippant references to *niggers* and *chinks*, now shocking, that were once second nature to writers like Rudyard Kipling. Use such non-PC terms today and doubts are raised about your basic moral commitments. If advocates of diversity insist that certain minority groups be named in particular ways, then the safest course is clearly the one that carries the PC stamp of approval.

Of course, if a particular group wants to be called by a certain name, then it also becomes a matter of simple civility. But then the question is, who decides on the name? Who decides the identity of a group, and its desires and interests? The PC battle often ends up being as much about who has the power to name, as the actual naming itself.

History of 'gay'

I don't know how often in phone-calls, emails and face-to-face conversations I have heard people remonstrating about the shift in meaning of the word *gay* from 'merry and bright' to 'homosexual'. But, in fact, since it first made its appearance in the English language in the 1300s, *gay* has held a multitude of different meanings. 'Bright, full of fun' was only ever one of these. The tangled history of the word offers us a wonderful illustration of just how complicated meaning shifts can be – and how flawed our thinking often is when it comes to etymology.

Very early in its history, *gay* started to be used euphemistically as a general term for those given to 'revelling and self-indulgence', as *The Oxford English Dictionary* delicately puts it. The male revellers of the 1600s were known as *gay dogs*. A *gay girl* was a 'strumpet' (not a 'lesbian'). *Gay* clearly had as one of its central meanings at this time 'sexually active'. But this meaning could well have been around much earlier than the Oxford citations suggest – perhaps even as early as medieval English. It's not clear to me that all these citations are the straightforward 'epithets of praise' that they appear to be, especially when applied to women. Many of the references to *gaye gerles* and *ladyes gay* are dripping in sexual innuendo.

Certainly by the time we get to the early 18th century, *gay* with the meaning 'promiscuous' was well and truly entrenched in the language, as also attested in the associated expressions *gay in the legs, groin* or *arse* referring to 'promiscuity', *the gaying instrument* 'the penis' and *to gay it* meaning 'copulate'. Of course, when applied to women, *gay* followed the usual path of these kinds of words and quickly took on moral overtones. It wasn't long before it had become a thoroughly negative word meaning 'promiscuous woman' or 'prostitute'. Our society has always attached quite different values to male and female sexuality and this causes female-specific words to acquire quite different evaluative loadings – comparable male terms are always less negative and remain more stable over time.

So far, these have all been heterosexual uses of the term *gay*. Indeed, most dictionaries don't cite the appearance of homosexual senses until into the 1920s. This is curious, since they were almost certainly around in earlier times. It would be strange if this weren't the case, since it is common for contemptuous terms for females to turn into terms of abuse for male homosexuals. English has many such examples. *Faggot*, for instance, was originally a pejorative term for women. In his history of swearing, Geoffrey Hughes describes an incident in 1889 dubbed the 'Cleveland Street Scandal' involving a homosexual brothel. During the court proceedings that followed there is a clear use of *gay* in reference to homosexuals.

More recent times (notably the 1960s) have seen a re-evaluation by both male and female homosexuals of the derogatory semantics of a number of words such as *gay*. In the mouths of speakers who have 'natural cover' it's always possible to reclaim pejorative language in this way, and the appropriation of *gay* by homosexuals has been very successful (indeed, more successful than are usual attempts at re-evaluating vocabulary). (The label 'natural cover' is Glen Loury's – he uses it to refer to speakers who, because of their group identity, are not presumed to have malign motives for expressing themselves in a potentially offensive way.) *Gay* meaning 'homosexual', as both noun and adjective, has now become generally accepted usage and this is indeed the dominant meaning. Since the 1960s the word has been used less and less in the sense 'bright, full of fun', and most speakers, catching themselves using the adjective *gay* in this earlier sense, will with some embarrassment explicitly draw attention to the intended meaning.

In her essay on political correctness, Peggy Noonan describes *gay* as once being 'a good word because it sounded like what it meant – "merry and bright"'. She also announces that she feels the need to 'rescue' the word and return it to its 'true meaning' –

all 'in the name of candor, courage, and coherence'. In fact, the etymology of *gay* can be traced back to one of two Old High German words – one with the meaning 'good' or 'beautiful', the other 'impetuous' or 'swift'. Modern wordsmiths seem to prefer the former, although it's still not at all clear which is the correct source. But I presume neither 'impetuous' nor 'swift' is the 'true meaning' Peggy Noonan had in mind! 'Merry, bright' is of course what she grew up with and feels comfortable with – and it's this meaning she wants to revive.

Clearly, words are nothing like those tight little bundles of form and meaning we imagine them to be. Natural language just doesn't work that way. Teenagers are already using *gay* in a quite different sense. A feature of their slang is to turn meanings of ordinary words on their heads and *gay* has now become a sneer term with roughly the meaning 'stupid'. It's not clear whether this slang will endure, but one thing is certain – the meaning of *gay* will not stand still.

Salt, silt, sausage and salad

During February 2002 in Mildura (a city in northern Victoria on the Murray River), a festival was held in celebration of 'salt' – the much awaited 'Salt Event'. There's no doubt that salt is an extraordinarily valuable commodity – indispensable to life, vital to the preservation of food and a delicacy in cooking. As the Goth administrator Cassiodorus said as early as the 5th century, 'It may be that some seek not gold, but there lives not a man that does not need salt'.

The fundamental importance of salt is very evident in phrases such as *worth one's salt*, an expression that derives from the original practice of paying in salt rather than in cash. Those who were worth their salt were 'capable' and 'competent', in other words, deserving of their pay. There's also the expression *salt of the earth* to refer to 'the most worthy of people'. This comes from Matthew 5: 13: 'Ye are the salt of the earth'. Many of these expressions are no longer current – *being true to one's salt, if the salt have lost its savour*, Shakespeare's *salt of youth* and *to eat salt with a person*, that is, 'to enjoy their hospitality'. The phrase *below the salt* isn't much in evidence any more, either. It refers to the original practice of putting the salt cellar at the top of the table near the place of honour, so that those of inferior status would always sit below the salt. In different languages around the world, you can find similar phrases – all attest to the value of salt.

But it's the term for the substance itself that is interesting. The basis of the word for 'salt' in all the major European languages is the root *sal-* – think of German *Salz*, Dutch *zout*, French *sel*, Italian *sale* and of course English *salt*. However, the roots of *salt* have also spread into an extraordinary array of linguistic contexts. English words as different as *silt, salary, salad, sauce, saucer, sausage,* and the verb *to souse* all contain the linguistic element 'salt', although very little of the actual sense of 'salt' remains.

Silt requires just a simple change of vowel – *salt* to *silt*. Originally a salty deposit, it has since generalized to any kind of earthy sediment carried by moving water. The word *salary* shows better the importance of salt. It derives from a Latin term for an allowance given to soldiers to pay for salt. Now, in the case of *salad*, the root sense of salt is evident in the nature of the all-important dressing, which was originally very, very salty. According to foodie and lexicographer John Ayto, the Romans were great salad-eaters. Their salads weren't all that different from ours today – a mixture of raw vegetables such as lettuce, endive and cucumber, and always with some sort of dressing of oil, vinegar or brine. In Vulgar Latin the name for this dish was actually *herba salata*, literally 'herb salted' from which comes our term *salad*.

The beloved *sausage* also goes back to Latin *sal* 'salt'. Apparently, the Romans used to stuff pounded meat, spices and herbs into a skin of animal intestine to form cylindrical rolls. It was a convenient way of keeping meat, and this salty preserving aspect is maintained in its name – *sausage*. The *sauce* you put on the sausage shares the root word too. Originally, sauces were any kind of appetizing condiment that accompanied food and it doesn't take much phonological imagination to see Latin *salsus* 'salted' still lurking there. The word *saucer* is also a close relative. Initially it was the receptacle on the table for holding the sauces or indeed the salt itself.

Apply another simple change of vowel and you get to the verb *to souse*. Sousing referred to the preparation and preservation of meat or fish by soaking or pickling it in vinegar or brine. Of course, nowadays it's generalized to mean simply 'to plunge into water or any kind of liquid' – although probably in our current English it more usually refers to drinking and intoxication. Someone who's soused is, after all, *pickled, canned, bottled, sozzled* or at least *well-marinated*. The metaphor lives on!

Now, Voltaire is reputed to have once said of etymology that it is a science in which consonants count for very little and vowels for nothing at all. It's probably apocryphal. Nonetheless, when you look at a collection of linguistic relatives like *salt, silt, salary, salad, sauce, saucer, sausage* and *souse* it's easy to understand why you might come to this conclusion. All these words are linked to 'salt', but years of vowel and consonant changes have obscured the connections, and years of meaning shifts have taken the words a long way from the root sense. Certainly, be wary – some etymological endeavours are fairly fanciful. But the links between these particular linguistic relatives are well established. In this instance, it's not necessary to take the customary pinch of salt.

Gad, goad, gadding about and the gad-fly

Some time back I had reason to check on the pedigree of two particular words – *gad* and *goad*. It had occurred to me they might somehow have a common origin. As it turns out, they don't, but their histories intertwine and overlap in intriguing ways.

Gad is an extremely old word. It's been around for at least a thousand years. The original meaning must have been something like 'spike' or 'rod'. It could also be a simple bar of metal and was once used as a measure of length. It's historically related to the word *yard*, but its clash with the word *goad* ended up influencing its development and taking it a long way from *yard*. *Goad* is also an old word. It happened to be similar sounding and have a close meaning, but it's not related historically to *gad*, or so the experts maintain. *Goad* is actually a relative of the Old English word *gar* meaning 'spear'. (This is the same *gar* as in *garlic* – *garlic* means literally 'spear-leek'.)

So both nouns *gad* and *goad* had the meaning of something that pricks or wounds; both were used for prodding or driving oxen, although *gad* didn't develop this sense until the 1300s. Obviously it must have been influenced here by *goad*. There were also phrases such as *upon the gad* (meaning 'suddenly, on the spur of the moment' – as if pricked by a *gad* or a *goad*). However, *goad* ended up taking on more the meaning of 'spur' or 'stimulus', and nowadays we use it typically as a verb meaning 'to incite'. As a noun, *goad* still exists as the spike for driving oxen or more generally as a stimulus, but it's definitely less usual than the verb. *Gad* doesn't exist with any of its earlier meanings. Today we use it only in the sense of rushing about from place to place, as in *gadding about*. So where does this sense come from?

Could it be the *gad-fly*? I felt sure gad-flies had to be involved somehow – but, disappointingly, this cannot be. *Gad-fly* appears to have grown out of the original sense of *gad* as a spiked tool or spear. Clearly, it's an appropriate name for the sort of fly that stings and goads cattle. It's tempting to think of the expression *gad about* as sprouting from this word *gad-fly* (sounds plausible to me – rushing around as if stung by a gad-fly). But the chronology is entirely wrong. *Gad-fly* didn't appear until the 1600s; so it's a much later word. *To gad* or *gad about* was around a couple of centuries earlier. *Gad-bees* appeared in the 1500s, but this is still not early enough for *gad* the verb. Even more problematic is the sense of the term. Originally, it was a much more laid-back verb. If you were *gadding* or *gadding about* in the 1400s you were just wandering around or roving idly with no particular purpose in mind. It doesn't seem to have had any of the sense of flitting about in an uncontrolled manner that it usually does today. (Another blow for my gad-fly theory!) Some etymologists suggest that this *gad* was a backformation from the word *gadling*, a word which meant 'vagabond'. Just to confuse matters, this *gadling* derives from yet another *gad* word – this time Old English *gæd* meaning 'fellowship' + *-ling* (the same suffix you get in words like *darling*). In other words, a *gadling* was originally 'someone belonging to a fellowship', 'a companion'.

Let me sum up. *Gad* and *goad* appear to have collided. They were always similar in pronunciation and meaning and so they also kept encroaching on each other's semantic territory. Of the two, only *goad* remains in Modern English, although *gad* lingers on in *gad-fly*. The verb *to gad* or *gad about* seems to come from a different *gad* again; this is the *gad* meaning 'fellowship', derived from *gadling* – so, nothing do with gad-flies. However, in speakers' minds the expressions *gad about* and *gad-fly* have obviously also collided. Undoubtedly it's the association with gad-flies that has caused the verb *gad about* to shift its meaning from 'wander idly' to 'rush around'.

All this is a fine example of what you so often discover in the history of words. Speakers are constantly making associations of sound and sense. Where there's similarity in sound and a relationship in meaning, then we infer that there is a kinship there. Words come to contaminate each other, both in shape and meaning. And sometimes, as in the example given here, the effects can be long-term. It's all part of our trying to make sense of language. I can certainly understand why *titivate* is currently shifting its meaning from 'spruce up' to 'excite agreeably'. Some combinations of sounds seem particularly well-suited to certain meanings and so we make them fit – there's just too much titillation in *titivate*!

Historical versus historic

One aspect of language that appears to irritate speakers particularly is the use of combinations of words that overlap or copy each other in meaning. This is tautology – saying what you've already said. It includes examples such as *past experience, invited guests* and many more everyday expressions. This sort of linguistic overkill also occurs in word derivation. Occasionally, two endings with what look to be the same grammatical meanings are added to the same word at the same time. For example, *ironic* versus *ironical, rhythmic* versus *rhythmical, problematic* versus *problematical*. In cases like these, the stacking up of endings with apparently identical functions doesn't appear to bring about any change in meaning. So why use the *-ical* ending in *ironical* when simply *-ic* will do? It looks like needless doubling up. Is it just a love of high-bred affixes that creates words like *ironical* and *rhythmical*? Are we just adding classically inspired endings for the sake of sounding more profound? Is it simply another example of the sort of linguistic pretentiousness that turns the act of salting your own hamburger into *autocondimentation*?

The *-ic* versus *-ical* question is a complicated one. So let me begin at the beginning. There are two sources for *-ical* words in English. Some come directly from late Latin adjectives formed from nouns ending in *-icus*. Hence, the Latin word *grammaticus*, meaning 'grammarian', gives *grammaticalis* and therefore English *grammatical*. In other words, examples like *grammatical* come ready-made into English from Latin. Other examples involve the addition of the *-al* ending, often onto nouns ending in *-ic*, as in *musical* from *music*. But there are also instances where the *-al* ending appears to be creating new adjectives from what are already adjectives. We have quite a number of such pairs, including *ironic* and *ironical*, *economic* and *economical*, *historic* and *historical*, *comic* and *comical*.

If you examine the history of word pairs like *ironic* and *ironical* you'll usually find that it's the *-ical* forms that have been in the language longer. So it's not a simple matter of wanting to sound more impressive. Nonetheless, the apparent doubling up does upset a number of people. And at first blush it does look like overkill. Why not simply opt for one form over the other – *ironical* is surely nonessential because *ironic* will do?

The problem is that there are a number of word pairs that *do* show a meaning distinction. As both the *Webster's* and *Oxford* dictionaries point out, the *-ic* adjectives such as *economic* usually have the sense of 'pertaining to'. For example, *comic* relates to the nature of comedy, as in *a comic actor*. *Economic* relates to 'the science of economics', as in *economic rationalism*. *Historic* means 'well-known' or 'recorded in history', as in *an historic event*. In other words, the *-ic* examples relate closely to the central meaning of the stem of the subject word. In keeping with this, you'll find that adjectives that derive from placenames, nationalities and languages only ever appear in the *-ic* forms; they don't have *-ical* counterparts. For example, *Baltic* or *Arabic*. Like *-ic* adjectives generally, these are more restricted in their meanings. The same goes for technical vocabulary. Adjectives such as *hypnotic* and *megalithic* have no *-ical* partners either – *hypnotical* and *megalithical* don't exist.

In contrast, the *-ical* forms have a more general sense of simply 'dealing with' or 'being connected somehow with' whatever appears in the stem of the word. So *comical* means 'funny or amusing', as in *a comical figure*. If you compare *a comical opera* with *a comic opera* the meaning difference becomes obvious. These *-ical* words can also have a whole heap of transferred senses; for instance, *an economical person* is 'one who is thrifty', *historical* means 'concerned with the study of history, or simply belonging to the past'. Clearly, for some pairs of *-ic* and *-ical* adjectives the meanings are significantly different. However, the differences are hard to maintain. You'll find that some speakers now use the *-ic* adjectives like *economic* and *historic* in the broader sense of their *-ical* relatives *economical* and *historical*. When words are very similar in form it's often difficult to keep their meanings apart, especially when these meanings overlap. Just look at *gad* and *goad* – or the current collision of *enormity* and *enormousness*, *titillate* and *titivate*.

Relics of *-ical*

Pairs of adjectives like *historic* and *historical* were once much more common but over time one of the forms dropped out of use. In the case of *rhetorical* and *rhetoric*, *rhetorical* won out. Phrases such as *rhetoric questions* and *rhetoric eloquences* are no longer possible. But with *tragic* and *tragical*, it was *tragic* that triumphed. Marlowe's 'Think not but I am tragical within' sounds very odd to modern ears. Now, as I've mentioned before, when an aspect of the language drops out of use it rarely disappears without leaving behind a relic of some sort. The remains of all these lost *-ical* adjectives are their adverb forms. Notice that the derived adverb from *tragic* is *tragically*, even though there's no longer an adjective *tragical*. An exception to this is the word *publical*. In Modern English, *public* is one of the few *-ic* adjectives that forms its adverb by simply adding *-ly*. In this case, the adjective *publical* has vanished without leaving a trace.

Disinterested versus uninterested

I was surprised when I looked up the word *disinterested* in my various dictionaries. In the *Macquarie* the central meaning listed was 'unbiased by personal involvement or advantage; not influenced by selfish motives'. The secondary meaning it gave was 'uninterested', in other words, 'lacking interest'. This meaning it labelled 'colloquial', but I suspect many would prefer the label 'wrong' rather than 'colloquial' here. Certainly there are a lot of English speakers who feel strongly that the difference in meaning between *uninterested* and *disinterested* should be upheld, and they see the dictionary as the place to do this. For these people *disinterested* should have the meaning 'impartial, neutral' as opposed to *uninterested* with the meaning 'having or showing no interest'. To lose this distinction is for some speakers an irritation.

It's not surprising that many speakers these days understand *disinterested* to be the negative form of *interested*. After all, the prefix *dis-* is commonly used to make adjectives negative. *Agreeable* becomes *disagreeable*; *tasteful* becomes *distasteful*; *interested* becomes *disinterested*. You might have noticed that some speakers actually use *disinterested* to convey a more emphatic sense of 'lacking interest' – for these people, it's a stronger word than *uninterested*. But I guess this is not the point for those who see the loss of the distinction between *uninterested* and *disinterested* as the result of pure ignorance. I believe, however, that this distinction has probably always been a bogus one.

According to the entry in *The Oxford English Dictionary* the earliest meaning of *uninterested* is actually 'unbiased, impartial'. This now obsolete sense first appeared in the early 1600s. The meaning we have today ('showing no interest or concern') didn't appear until more than 100 years later. Even more surprising is the entry for *disinterested*. The first meaning given for this word is, no, not 'unbiased, impartial' but rather 'without concern, not interested' – precisely the meaning that is condemned by so many today. This meaning was around as early as 1612, so it can hardly be described as a recent and ignorant misuse, since it's clearly been a central sense of *disinterested* right from the beginning. In short, it seems that what *The Macquarie Dictionary* now describes as the central sense of the word *disinterested* (namely, 'unbiased, impartial') came later. The so-called colloquial sense 'without interest or concern' is in fact older, albeit only slightly. Furthermore, the current central sense of the word *uninterested* ('showing no interest or concern') came later too. Recall that *uninterested* first appeared with the meaning 'unbiased, impartial'.

In other words, *uninterested* and *disinterested* appear to have swapped places!

Even allowing for the fact that the dates in the dictionary rely on first appearances in writing and therefore may not be wholly accurate, clearly the point is this – both *disinterested* and *uninterested* have been sharing senses from the very beginning. There has never been a clear distinction between the two, as people are claiming today. And there's no problem with this. The word *disinterested* can hold at once both meanings 'impartial' and 'lacking interest'. After all, the vast majority of our words have more than one meaning and there's no problem – context is usually enough to make the sense clear.

Word forms and meanings are constantly changing, more so than any other aspect of language, and this must be a real problem for lexicographers. When does a word or a meaning become dictionary-worthy? But the sense of the word *disinterested* that the *Macquarie* describes as colloquial and the *Oxford* as 'a loose use' has been in the language for nearly 400 years – I think it's time these descriptions were revised. Indeed, in this regard my *Webster's* is bravely up-to-date in listing 'not interested' as the first sense of *disinterested*. However, the editors do provide a lengthy explanation for the benefit of those readers who 'may not fully appreciate the history of this word or the subtleties of its present use'.

Interested parties

 At the risk of boring the socks off you, can I make one final point with respect to this pair of words, *disinterested* and *uninterested*? It has always struck me as curious that those who rail against the current misuse of *disinterested* don't notice that the word *interested* has precisely the same potential ambiguity. The more usual meaning of *interested* is 'having concern, curiosity or enthusiasm for something', as in *They are interested students and keen to learn*. However, it can also have the meaning 'having a stake in something' as in *Interested parties should make a*

written submission. I'm not aware of any confusion that results from the fact that *interested* now holds these two different senses. In fact, both have been part and parcel of the meaning of the word since it first appeared in the English language in the 1600s.

Gravy train

A lot of folk appear to be riding gravy trains at the moment. Everywhere in the news we read about people who are deriving advantages from what appear to be rather overpaid but also undemanding tasks – and often it's some sort of government gravy train that's being ridden. This term *gravy train* got me wondering. How long have people been riding gravy trains and how on earth did this expression arise?

Perhaps I should begin at the beginning with the word *gravy* itself. It's an odd word in English, being what is known as a 'ghost word' – a word that doesn't really exist. In this case, it's a word that came about because of a blunder, specifically a scribal blunder. The word derives from Old French, either *graine* meaning 'meat' or *grané* meaning 'grain of spice'. You see, the original gravy was nothing like our modern-day gravy – it was more like a sauce made from broth, thickened with almonds and usually very heavy with spices and herbs (often to disguise the smell and flavour of rotting meat). Something known as *grany bastard* apparently was an inferior version of this sauce made with breadcrumbs rather than ground almonds. Anyway, sometime during the 14th century someone slipped up in translating the original French cook books and misread the 'n' of the French word – and the mistake stuck. So instead of pronouncing this word as 'graney', which is how we should pronounce it, the word came into English as *grav(e)y* – and when a ghost word such as this one makes its appearance in writing, it's usually impossible to flush it out.

By the 17th century the nature of *gravy* itself was changing – it was starting to look more like the modern-day gravy made from juices produced by roasting meat. It fact, during this time it became quite an elaborate affair, with special cuts of meat being used specifically for this purpose, hence our term *gravy beef*, that part of the leg cooked simply for the sake of its gravy. You can see how the term might then come to be applied metaphorically for 'a pleasant bonus, something desirable and perhaps unexpectedly acquired' – the gravy is, after all, a rather pleasant accompaniment to the food, a desirable dressing. Of course, to understand this metaphorical shift you really have to put aside all thoughts of that revolting, muddy brown lubricant for meat that became popular during the early part of the 20th century – this was made from powder or some sort of freeze-dried gravy granules. Metaphor is supposed to involve the perception of similarity between an object and an abstract concept – it's hard to imagine any connection between this culinary quagmire and something desirable. Yet, it would seem that the Great British Gravy, as it was sometimes known, was seen for the most part as a delicious extra, and this is what triggered the shift from 'appetizing sauce or dressing' to 'unearned or unexpected bonus'. This must also have occurred sometime in the early 20th century. *The Oxford English Dictionary* gives as its first entry a quote from 1910. It reads, 'Stick him for all you can. You're a hard worker, and you mustn't let some-body else git the gravy' (sic). From here it's not difficult to get to expressions like *ride* (or *board*) *the gravy train* (or *boat*) and from there to *gravy train*, meaning 'sinecure' or, as one dictionary puts it, 'easy money especially from a well-paid but undemanding task in political life or with a large company'. This use is first recorded in 1927 as American slang – from here it spread widely in the English-speaking world.

For centuries scholars have been trying to describe and explain meaning shifts. It's undoubtedly the most complex part of our language, probably because more than any other area, it's tied to the cultural and social aspects of a speech community. All sorts of wild things drive these changes and they can take words down remarkable paths. Clearly, in this instance, the *gravy train* has come a very long way from the original medieval mixture of broth, almond meal and spices that made up gravy during that period. We might know a lot about linguistic change, but I doubt we'll ever be able to reliably predict the tracks that words can travel with respect to their meanings.

Why gravy?

Let me explain a little more about how scribes could have misread *gravey* for *graney*. The problem was that the letters u, v, i, m and n were all very similar at this time. The strokes were identical. To make matters worse, scribes didn't leave a space between the letters. So if you had a whole lot of them together it was extremely difficult to figure out what they represented. Let's say you had five strokes in a row. That could represent uni, uvi, imi, ivu, nui and a number of other possibilities. Things were made even harder because it wasn't the custom then to put a dot or a stroke above the letter 'i'. Small wonder there was the occasional slip.

Incidentally, it was this same confusion over letters that triggered some rather peculiar spelling changes by the French scribes of the time. Thinking it would make life easier, they developed the convention of writing a 'u' as an 'o' in those words where two or three of these tricky letters appeared in sequence. This is why we have spelling anomalies in Modern English like *love, honey, come, son* and *one* – these were originally written with 'u', much like *butter, crumb* and *summer*.

Proving the rule

When meanings of individual words shift, you often find relics of their earlier senses stuck in longer expressions. English is full of lexical curiosities of this nature. Take the phrase *the exception that proves the rule*. How most people understand it these days is this: here is an exception that confirms the rule. This is hardly surprising, given that *prove* usually means 'to establish the truth of something'. The problem here is that the meaning of *prove* has changed. When it first appeared in the phrase it meant 'try or put to the test'. This meaning is retained in related words like *proof*, as in *the proof of the pudding*. So we really should understand this expression as meaning that the rule is being tested – here's an exception and it calls into question the validity of the rule. It's tricky when words change their meanings. Outdated senses often get left behind in this way, and this can then render such fixed expressions nonsensical. Why on earth would an exception confirm a rule; surely it brings the rule into question? But speakers do their darnedest to make sense of the phrase and, when I was younger, I always made sense of this one by assuming that, well, rules were meant to be broken. So for something to be a rule there had to be at least one exception.

One solution, then, is to reinterpret these anomalous phrases and give them new meanings. Another oddity that puzzled me as a child is the expression *more haste less speed*. The earliest meaning of *speed* – from the 8th century in fact – is 'success, prosperity, profit'. The phrase *good speed* meant at that time 'good fortune'. In those days if you wished someone 'good speed', you weren't referring to a rapid rate of movement. So that curious phrase *more haste less speed* makes a good deal more sense with the earlier meaning of *speed* as 'success'; in other words, more haste brings about less success. Before I'd realized the earlier meaning of *speed*, I had simply assumed that because *haste* also had an element of impetuousness or rashness, hasty actions therefore ultimately meant a slower rate of movement. It made sense for me.

A lot of old quotations get reinterpreted in this way. For example, ask people nowadays what they understand by *hoist by his own petard*. Usually they'll talk about someone being strung up by his own rope. There are two problems here. One is that *petard* has virtually disappeared from ordinary usage. It doesn't mean much to us any more, but originally it was some sort of war-like explosive device used, for example, to blow up a wall. It was much like a mine, but a rather badly made one, it would seem, because frequently it also blew up the soldier who was using it. *Petard* is in fact related to the word *fart* – it comes from a French verb meaning 'to break wind'.

The other problem with being *hoist by your own petard* is the now obsolete meaning of *hoist*, namely 'to lift and remove' or 'to bear away'. If petards were involved, it entailed being blown up by your own bomb. These days we usually understand *hoist* to mean simply lifting or raising, as in a sail or a flag. So it's easy to reinterpret this expression to mean being strung up by one's own rope. (A subtle change of preposition helps this version – Hamlet's original was *hoist **with** his own petar*.) In this instance, however, the general meaning remains the same. It doesn't matter whether bombs or ropes are involved, you're still being caught out by your own device.

As a final example, take the very common expression *to beg the question*. This is certainly one that's currently shifting in meaning. Originally it referred to the practice of assuming something that implies the conclusion or, as *The Macquarie Dictionary* more elegantly puts it, 'to assume the point that is being raised in the question'. An example often given is to say something like 'parallel lines will never meet because they're parallel' – this begs the question because you've assumed exactly the thing you set out to prove. But this is not how *beg the question* is often used these days. Many people understand it now to mean something more general, as in 'to raise the question'. In fact, *The Macquarie Dictionary* has this exact meaning at the end of its entry for *beg*. The editors point out that their corpus evidence shows that this meaning is gaining currency. Presumably this has come about because the original meaning assumed a rather unusual understanding of the verb *beg* 'to take for granted without warrant', as the *Oxford* entry puts it. Since the general understanding of *beg* is 'to ask for', it's hardly surprisingly that speakers have reinterpreted the phrase *beg the question* as meaning 'raise the question'.

So, is all this misuse? Some would certainly think so. But it's the old problem – when does misuse become use? To take the earlier example, do millions of native speakers of English misuse the word *speed* because really it means 'success', as it did in the 8th century? When a few people start using *beg the question* to mean 'raise the question', then it's clearly misuse. But when many people start using the phrase this way, what do you do? You can't fine them. You can't flog them. And even if you could, it's unlikely to do any good. Suddenly, most of the population are using *beg the question* to mean 'raise the question'. Unfortunately, there's no magic time when misuse becomes use. It's murky and it's messy.

Gaps in our vocabulary

The vocabulary of a language, especially the relative volume of words clustering around particular concepts or things, always provides interesting clues as to what might or might not be significant within a speech community. The Anglo-Saxons, for instance, were a particularly bellicose bunch and not surprisingly Old English had a remarkably rich lexicon for war and death that captured distinctions no longer possible (perhaps fortunately) in the modern language.

It's also clear that a language can sometimes discriminate against certain of its speakers in this way. There might be gaps, for example. Take specific words relating to the sexes. There is, for instance, no word in English to denote specifically female heroic qualities. *Virago* once did, but like so many female-associated terms, it has since acquired quite negative connotations. From the meaning 'heroic woman, female warrior' it quickly deteriorated to 'scold, shrew; noisy, domineering, thoroughly dislikeable woman'. For many speakers, the word was anyway never totally satisfactory, since it actually meant 'manlike' and didn't refer to heroism in a woman's own right. Much like the word *virtue*, *virago* is based on the Latin word for 'male person' – *vir*.

There are other curious gaps in English too. Someone once asked me if we had a term meaning 'pertaining to an aunt', parallel to *avuncular*. As far as I know, we don't. The Latin terms for 'aunt' haven't left their mark on English in the way that *avunculus* did. In fact, there are many such imbalances in our Latin-based terms. We have a word *uxoricide* that refers specifically to 'wife-killing'. It seems there's no equivalent word for the killing of a husband. Perhaps this particular gap doesn't worry you, but it is odd. It's not as if husband-killers are unknown in history. This grisly act has always fallen under the umbrella term *parricide*, a word that refers generally to the killing of a close relative. There was one early candidate: the word *viricide*. It could have stepped in to plug the hole, except that since the early 20th century *viricide* has been used for the killing of viruses, not husbands. So the gap remains. Now, if you feel the need to introduce a term for husband-killing, Latin has another word for 'husband', *maritus*, which would then give us *mariticide* (not to be confused with *matricide* 'mother-killing'). Occasionally gaps are filled in this way. For instance, since the early 17th century English has had the terms *misogynist* and *misogyny* to refer to the hatred of women, as well as the all-purpose terms *misanthrope* and *misanthropy* for the general dislike of people. However, there was no term to refer specifically to the hatred of men – that is until the early 20th century when *misandry* plugged the hole. A 'hater of men' would therefore be a *misandrist*.

Now, many feminists have complained that there are also systematic gaps in English for words relating specifically to female sexual experiences. Verbs referring to sexual intercourse appear either neutral (like *to have sex, have intercourse*) or they require a male subject (like *to ejaculate, penetrate*). There are also no expressions that refer to female sexual potency – for example, no female equivalent of *virility* (or *emasculate*, for that matter). On the other hand, what you do find is a collection of words for sexually promiscuous women that far outnumbers those for males. Over the years English has amassed an extraordinary 2,000 derogatory expressions akin to *slut* and *slag*. Not only is the list considerably smaller for men, but the words are also far less negative. There's nothing of the same pejorative sense of sexual promiscuity. Clearly, our society places very different values on male and female sexuality and this is reflected in these sorts of asymmetries in our vocabulary.

But changes are afoot. Derogatory expressions like *whore, bitch* and *slut* that have traditionally applied only to females and gay males are now being used, by some speakers at least, across the board. Also telling is the recent appearance of terms like *he-man, hunk, jock, beefcake, stud, stud muffin* and so on. Alongside *bimbo* we now find *himbo* for the male who is ruggedly handsome, well-built (but with usually very little between the ears). So whereas expressions for the physical attributes of women usually far exceed those available for describing men, what we're now seeing is a proliferation of equivalent 'brawn' terms for males. And as lexicographer Geoffrey Hughes points out, there has also been an increase in negative terms for those antithetical male types like *nerd, wimp, weed, wuss, drip* and *wet*. Social upheaval generally does have linguistic repercussions, and it's not surprising that recent changes to women's place in society are having an impact on our vocabulary. Certainly it appears that some of the imbalances are now being redressed. But there's a disturbing trend here, too, and one that also shows up in meaning shifts elsewhere. Just look at the way words such as *image* and *model* are currently changing. *Image* 'representation' becomes 'cultivated favourable public reputation'. *Model* 'ideal example' becomes the glamorous and sexually attractive clothes-horse we see on the catwalks. It's our general obsession with appearance and physical attributes that is also driving the lexical changes we're seeing here.

Witches, wizards and warlocks

One reason we have so many derogatory expressions for women is that words with female application deteriorate over time. Compare, for example, terms to do with witchery and wizardry.

The first recorded uses of *witch* denoted a man who practised witchcraft, in other words, a sorcerer, a wizard. References to male witches were around as early as 890, but by the year 1000 it was used of women and had become something very nasty. A *witch* was a female who had dealings with the devil and so possessed occult and evil powers. Our rather jokey image of witches these days makes it hard for us to imagine the potency of this word in early times. And while this potency waned as belief in witchcraft declined, the term never completely shed its connotations of evil. We still retain abusive epithets like *old witch* and expressions like *witches' cauldron* to describe some kind of sinister situation.

Wizard was originally also synonymous with evil, but by the 17th century it was being used figuratively, with positive connotations, for someone who could perform wondrous acts: a man skilful in his profession. *The Macquarie Dictionary* now defines *wizard* as 'someone of exceptional or prodigious accomplishment (especially in a specified field)'. As a slang term *wizard* is still heard to mean 'marvellous, superb' and the noun *wizardry* refers to 'skill or expertise'. I am told that in the computer world a *wizard* is also a small program or set of instructions that gives you a short-cut and easy guide to what may otherwise be a complex task.

Like *wizard*, *warlock* was also synonymous with evil and maliciousness, but once again since the 1700s it has lost these associations. Though not used terribly often today, most of us would understand *warlock* in the milder sense of 'magician or conjurer'.

The histories of words such as *shrew, scold, dragon, termagant, siren, harpy* and *hag* tell a similar story. All have narrowed to female application alone. Shrews were once rascals and scolds were poets. And though the senses of these words have clearly weakened over time, they continue to epitomize misogynist views.

Name-dropping

Clearly there will always be a close relationship between social change and semantic change. Shifts in societal mores or attitudes will typically have semantic correlatives. Consider the shifts in meaning that are currently taking place in words such as *celebrity* ('a solemn religious ceremony' to 'popular public figure'), *charisma* ('divinely conferred power' to 'popular aura'), *cult* ('system of religious worship' to 'popular fashion involving devotion to a person or thing') and *personality* ('pertaining to the person' to 'popular public figure'). There are also the shifts I alluded to earlier – *image* ('representation of person/thing' to 'cultivated favourable public reputation') and *model* ('representation of person/thing' to 'ideal representation' to 'person employed to display clothing'). These shifts are strongly suggestive of a culture that's becoming increasingly shallow and self-centred. Many of these words, you'll notice too, have been stripped of their religious significance with the growing secularization of English-speaking societies. Geoffrey Hughes' book *Words in Time* offers a social history of English vocabulary and many of the semantic changes he documents in it tell a similar story.

The egotistical nature of modern-day success also shows itself in the way we behave with regard to names. In contrast to past times, our media-conscious Western world has become a culture that busily promotes personal names. Everyone, it seems, is out there striving to *be a name*. Name-dropping is believed to give us social clout. People dispose of their names and adopt new ones to promote a better public image. People can even sell their names. When well-known people endorse commercial products they're flogging their names. Those that buy the product often expect to pay more to have that particular name inscribed on the goods. We use numerous phrases like *make a name for oneself, have a good name, bring one's name into disrepute, clearing one's name* and so forth.

The significance of personal names in our society also shows up in the ability of some names to lose their capital letter and enter the general lexicon as household words. These are eponyms (from *epi-* 'upon' and *onym* 'name'). What was once somebody's name becomes a common noun or verb. There are the older eponyms, of course – *cardigans* and *sandwiches* from the Earls of Cardigan and Sandwich. We've been doing this sort of thing for centuries and we have now amassed a surprising 35,000 of these expressions. Even more telling, I believe, are those eponymic phrases that arise spontaneously in our everyday language. Recently I heard someone refer to a popular singer as 'having done an Elvis' (in other words, this singer was so outstanding as to have achieved demi-god status). If you cook at home you may well now be described as 'doing a Delia'. Most are short-lived, it's true, but there's a rich abundance of such expressions these days.

How different this seems from those societies where there are strict taboos on naming! In many traditional communities 'true' names are actually secret, and euphemistic names are necessary for any public naming and addressing. The closest we come to taboos on 'true' names are the restrictions on naming *God* or *Christ*, but even these are now observed inconsistently.

Whether we reveal them or conceal them, personal names have extraordinary significance. Clearly, there is a very special relationship held between them and the individuals who bear them. Think of the difficulty that many speakers experience when they have to say out loud their own name. This does not only apply to children. Is it a vestigial superstition at revealing one's real name? Or is it simply that names are so inextricably bound up with our innermost selves that we feel embarrassed to reveal such an intimate detail to strangers? We *are* our names. When people misspell our names, they touch a soft spot. Insulting names do wound. Names aren't just symbols but are verbal expressions of our personalities – and to offend them is as great a blow as physical assault.

More name magic

 Another aspect to 'name magic' is the way we react to the personal names of strangers. Of course, names do come and go. So once popular names (such as Jason and Kylie) might reveal something of the age of a person. There are also traditional names (such as Susan and John) and novelty names (such as Sky and River). These may help us to assess the attitudes of the name bearer, or perhaps more so those of their parents. But studies of people's reactions to names also reveal that many of us go beyond this and actually link names with personalities. This is all part of our general stereotyping behaviour. Certain names make us recall the personality of individuals that also have that name. The name then somehow seems to fit that personality: Marys are quiet, Davids are strong, Kylies are sexy. When we encounter that name in a stranger, it generates a certain expectancy. It becomes one of the clues we use to access information about that person's social background or personality. Such stereotypes can be positive, negative, accurate or completely wrong-headed. But they are all of them selective. If you've come to associate certain personality traits with a certain name, when you encounter a person with that name, then you'll see what you want to see. The features you take note of will be those that confirm your expectations. They overshadow other features and become, for you, the main characteristics of that person. In fact, studies of stereotyping show that people will even go beyond the information they're given. They see features that aren't there at all, and fail to see ones that are.

For centuries people have believed in the supernatural abilities of names. Onomancy, for instance, refers to the practice of interpreting names as omens. Their meaning or their value in numerical terms is used to foretell future events or the destinies of their owners. There are probably few of us today who would admit to believing in the magical powers of names. Yet there is plenty of evidence to suggest that names still hold a special mystique for many people. After all, when we buy that tennis racket with the autograph on it, there must be some sort of name magic going on. Occasional punters at the race-track will often select a horse simply because its name holds some special significance. How many horses have I backed in the Melbourne Cup because their names were linked with a recent event or significant person in my life? Recently I typed the keywords 'name' and 'magic' into my computer web search engine. What turned up was extraordinary – instructions on how to cast a spell on someone using their 'true' name, how to find the luckiest name for a new born baby, how to find the perfect soul mate (using names and numerology to compute the emotional,

sexual and intellectual compatibility of you and your partner).
There are even sites that will assist you in finding meaningful
anagrams of your names as a way of interpreting your destiny. I
typed in my name and got 'a big rude trek' – hate to think what this
portends!

Words ending in *-gry*

What is the longest word in the English language? The most frequently used? What words have letters that occur three times in a
row? And what is that elusive word that rhymes with *orange*?
Well, I suppose it beats counting sheep if you're trying to sleep.
There are many curious and totally useless queries about the
English language that people collect and use to taunt others.
They're not really weeds, it's true. But like weeds they have a
peculiar fascination for us – and they're certainly pesky enough to
warrant a place in this book.

There is one such that crops up on a regular basis. Perhaps
quiz masters ask it, or it's used in trivia nights or word games. It's
certainly one I am frequently faced with. It's this: what is the
third word in the English language that ends in *-gry*? There's
angry, there's *hungry*, but what is the other one?

I gather this was originally a riddle, and there are a number of
different renditions of it. If you're interested, the magazine
Ozwords from the Australian National Dictionary Centre dis-
cusses a number of them in various 1997 and 1998 issues. The
clue always lies in the framing of the original question. For example, listener Tom Hogarth reminded me of the following (rather
curious) version: 'There are only three words in the English language that end in *-gry*: 1. Angry. 2. Hungry. 3. ? The word is one
that everyone uses every day and knows what it stands for. If
you've listened very carefully I've already told you what it is.
What is it?' The clue is in the second last sentence. In telling the
riddle, the speaker would have deliberately dropped the 'h' in
hungry. Hence, the third word is actually *'ungry*. That's all very
well and good, but I spent hours and hours dredging up obscure
English words ending in *-gry*. So I'm going to share with you my
findings, whether you like it or not.

There are an extraordinary number of these words, it turns out. Most are either obsolete or else dialectal – perhaps still surviving in some far away picturesque part of rural Britain or some remote area in the American South. Not many of them are terribly handy, although a couple of them do have potential. On the linguistic website LinguistList, Arlet Otten published a list of around a hundred of these *-gry* words – I should add, his list appeared well after I had spent days ploughing through dictionaries and bizarre vocabulary collections. He did come up with a few that I'd missed, although some are compounds built around *angry* and *hungry*, so I'm not sure I would allow these. A number are proper names, too. These I certainly wouldn't count. I probably wouldn't allow archaic spellings, either, of words like *savagery, imagery* and *buggery*, which all at some stage in their history have been spelt with *-gry*. Nonetheless, even if you take out the dubious cases, a substantial number are left. And I've checked every one on Otten's list. They do, or did once, all exist. Here are just some.

The first two are rather nice – *aggry*, an obscure word used in Victorian times to refer to coloured beads found buried in Africa; and also *iggry*, a very old army slang term meaning 'hurry up'. A couple are medical – *podagry* apparently was a 17th-century word for gout and *pottingry* some sort of strange corruption of the word *apothecary*. Not surprisingly, these words have never made it into our everyday vocabulary and have simply shuffled off the lexical coil. As has *congry* or *conygry*, an early word for rabbit warren. Since we lost the word *coney* meaning 'rabbit', it's not surprising that *conygry* went with it. One I rather like is a variant of *angry*, namely, *nangry*. This dates from the 17th century, a time when it was very common for boundaries between words to shift around. Often the 'n' of a preceding word such as *an* attached itself to what followed. So 'an angry man' might become 'a nangry man'. It was around this time that *nidiot* appeared as a common spelling for *idiot*. Both these dropped by the wayside, of course, but they do retain their entries in *The Oxford English Dictionary*. And indeed, some of these mistakes did survive. Our words *nickname, newt* and the personal name *Ned* got their 'n' that way.

There is a handful of these ancient *-gry* words that I feel might be worth resuscitating. *Huggry muggery* or *hoggry moggry* is a lovely way of saying 'disorderly, slovenly, confused'. I also quite like the dialect word *skugry* meaning 'secrecy', and Yorkshire *shiggry* meaning 'unwell' or 'drunken'. Also from Yorkshire comes *rungry* meaning 'strong, lusty, boisterous'. *Meagry* is rather lovely too – 'having a meagre appearance', as in *a pale and meagry child*. But one of these forgotten words really should be brought back to life and that is the word *gry*. It was a most versatile little word. Firstly, it referred to a hundredth of an inch in the old imperial system. OK, not terribly handy any more. But it could also denote the grunt of pig. A tad more useful, and you could imagine all sorts of extended uses here. But its third meaning, I feel, does genuinely fill a gap in our lexicon – *gry* 'dirt under the finger nail'. Now, that *is* a useful word. I can see all sorts of associated uses here, including the fluffy lint that gathers in your belly button. From there it could be extended to any small, insubstantial thing or trifle. This word *gry* has potential, and does deserve to be the third word in the English language that ends in *-gry*!

Before I finish here, let me leave you with another question. What is the third word in the English language that ends in *–shion*? There's *cushion*, there's *fashion* and there's at least one other. The answer can be found at the end of this book.

More curiosities

 Are there any English words where 'q' is not followed by 'u'? Technically, no. The spelling 'qu' was a Latin convention introduced by French scribes to replace the Old English spelling 'cw' and, with the exception of trade names like *Qantas* and borrowings like Chinese *qi* (the energy that flows through all things) and French *coq* as in *coq au vin*, there are no English words where 'q' appears without a following 'u'. The only contender might be *qwerty*, a word derived from the first six letters on the top left of an English-language typewriter; *qwerty* describes any keyboard that has this arrangement. (Of course there are also those obsolete spellings — for example, *qhat* and *qheche* for *what* and *which* — that some sneaky Scrabble players might try to get away with!)

Are there words in the English language that have the same letter three times in a row? Now, I'm not sure whether you would count these, but you will find three or even more of the same letters in some of those sound-symbolic words that represent involuntary noise responses like *shhh*, *hmmm* and *brrrr*. Or even *zzz* to indicate sleep! But usually the rules of English spelling, such as they are, don't allow for more than two of the same letters in a row. Someone who sees is a *seer* with two, and not three, 'e's. Or, if the word formation process does throw more than two such letters together, we typically write them with a hyphen – some dictionaries might have entries such as *frillless* ('lacking a frill') and *headmistressship*, but I'm sure you'd prefer these words spelt with a hyphen to break up the consonants.

Of course, if you include early spellings in this word game, then you let in a whole host of possibilities such as *uuular* for 'uvular' and *virtuuus* for 'virtuous'. And, if obsolete words are allowed, then my *Oxford English Dictionary* has a beauty – an entry with the extraordinary spelling *esssse*, a now forgotten word for 'ashes'. If you're interested in linguistic curiosities, here's one for your list. Surely four 's's in a row must win some sort of linguistic award!

Our Grammatical Weeds

There is an area I have been avoiding for months. Infested
with masses of rope twitchgrass and spreading rapidly too.
Preparations have been made. I have brought four punnets of
African marigolds, the big, vigorous ones called Crackerjack.
After grunting and digging my way through the root-ridden
soil and forking out as much of the twitch as possible, I squirt
holes with the hose jet . . . A few minutes later, when the water
has soaked away, in go the marigold seedlings, the great twitch
destroyer, five to the square metre. I could swear I hear the
twitch roots which still remain, squeaking with fear. What
a lovely way to start the summer.

Peter Cundall *Seasonal Tasks for the Practical*
Australian Gardener 1989

To dive deep or to dive deeply?

Adverbs form one of the motliest groups of all our parts of speech.
Their name 'adverb' suggests something quite straightforward –
adverbs are those words we use to modify verbs. In something like
he drove slowly, slowly modifies the verb *drive*. But adverbs can also
be used to modify other modifiers. In *he drove unbelievably slowly,*
unbelievably modifies the adverb *slowly*. In *an unbelievably slow*
driver, unbelievably modifies the adjective *slow*. Then there are
those adverbs that don't seem to modify anything at all. In an
example such as *Frankly, he's a twit*, the adverb *frankly* provides
more a comment on what's contained in the rest of the sentence.

In Modern English the earmark of our adverbs has become the
-ly ending, and when it's left off it's usually condemned as 'bad
English' as in *Drive slow*. Examples like this are usually thought to
be horrid neologisms, further evidence of the decline and decay of
our modern language. Often they're blamed on outside influences,

but in fact adverbs without the expected *-ly* ending are very old. They're certainly not a recent arrival on the scene. Here's a brief history that might explain why they have become such outlaws.

Around a thousand years ago, forming adverbs was quite straightforward. Most of the time they were derived from adjectives by the addition of a simple ending – a final vowel *e*. For instance, you could take the adjective *glaed* (the same as our modern word *glad*) and add an *-e* – *glaede* meaning 'gladly'. Now, the *-ly* ending on *gladly* that has become a feature of our modern adverbs was originally a noun *lic*, meaning 'body' or 'shape'. It's the same word *lych* 'body or corpse' that is preserved in Modern English *lychgate*, 'the gateway before the churchyard where a coffin is put down before burial'. This word *lic* was added to nouns in Old English to form adjectives. So from a noun like *craeft* meaning 'skill', you would form the adjective *craeflic* meaning literally 'having the appearance of skill', or 'skilful'. To make the adverb from these adjectives you would, as in other cases, simply add the *-e* onto the *lic* ending; hence *craeflic* 'skilful' became *craeftlice* 'skilfully'. It was clear-cut. However, language never stands still. What followed were the usual processes of reduction and omission – very familiar episodes in the story of English. In this instance, they had quite a dramatic effect.

It's another fact of lexical life that endings erode over time. By the end of the 14th century, the adverb-forming *-e* ending had virtually disappeared. Its loss is the reason we have adverbs today that have no ending at all and are identical to their adjectival form. These include words such as *fast, hard* – and yes, *slow*. So something like *Drive slow* is a kind of relic. You could think also of Shakespeare's 'grievous sick', 'wondrous strange' and 'indifferent cold'; Jonathan Swift's 'Your ale is terrible strong'; Rudyard Kipling's 'I'm awful sorry'. We wouldn't want to accuse Shakespeare, Swift or Kipling of 'bad English', but nowadays these examples do sound perfectly horrible to most modern Standard English ears. The problem is, of course, these bare adverbs have now fallen from grace.

The next episode in the erosion tale concerns wear and tear on the adjective-forming *lic* ending. With time, this was eventually reduced to our modern-day *-ly* suffix. This is why today we have a number of adjectives that end in *-ly* like *friendly*, as in *a friendly person*. But over the years, speakers gradually came to view this *-ly* ending as the natural way to form adverbs, even though this wasn't

It's like history repeating itself

There's another interesting wrinkle in all this. Not only did the Anglo-Saxon word *lic*, meaning 'body or shape', give rise to our Modern English *-ly* ending, as in *godly*, it also gave us the word *like* meaning 'of the same shape'. This means that the word *like* in the phrase *like a god*, or at the end of the word *godlike*, has the same origin as the *-ly* ending in *godly*. So, when speakers first created *godlike* in the 1500s, they were using the identical word-formation process that speakers had used centuries before to create *godlice* (the ancester of modern *godly*). It's a wonderful example of linguistic history repeating itself. You might also bear in mind that Anglo-Saxon *lic* is at the root of modern colloquial *like* in *It's like so excellent* or *I'm like gimme a break, will ya*. This *like* therefore has the same linguistic pedigree as *-ly* and also as the *lych* in *lychgate*. All of these various off-springs of Old English *lic* share the same general sense of 'resemblance' or 'similarity', and if you look hard enough you will still see remnants of the original meaning 'body, spirit' lurking there. It's a splendid illustration of the extraordinary way that words can evolve.

its original job description. You see, the disappearance of the original *-e* ending meant that the distinction between the forms *lic* and *lice* collapsed – both became simply *-ly*. This change meant that speakers were free to associate *-ly* with adverbs, and the pattern *slow–slowly* and *quick–quickly* became fixed as the model for forming adverbs in the modern standard language. So, before you condemn a speaker for saying 'Drive slow' or 'he ran quick', bear in mind these bare adverbs have been in continuous use for centuries.

Collective nouns

One of the many puzzling aspects of English grammar is the messy business of collective nouns and what to do about agreement. By agreement, I mean how we match the words in a sentence with respect to their number: whether they are singular or plural. Collectives are terms such as *government* and *public* that are singular in appearance, and yet they regularly appear with plural verbs. You commonly read in newspapers, for instance, that *the government **are** in a tricky position* or *the public **are** united on this*. So which is correct? Should that be *the government **is** in a tricky position* and *the public **is** united on this*?

It depends on your interpretation. A word like *government* is certainly a grammatically singular term, yet it can be understood in different ways. *Government* refers to a body or group that comprises a number of members. So it really depends on whether you're emphasizing the collective entity or its individual members. If you say *the government **has** made a decision*, then you're probably picturing a group of people who are of one mind. If you say *the government **have** made a decision*, the picture you have is probably more a group of individuals who have all independently arrived at the same decision.

However, it's not entirely a matter of semantics. There's plenty of regional variation, and certainly American and British usage is divided here. British speakers are much more likely to go for the plural option. Americans go more for the singular option. And as usual we Australians fall somewhere in the middle, although we do seem to be siding increasingly with the British. On the basis of a recent quick survey of Australian newspapers by my students, it appears the plural is much more common these days, at least in journalist-speak. However, there's a further complicating factor. The question of whether or not to use the plural doesn't arise only in respect to the following verb. It also crops up when you find yourself using a pronoun. Do you say *the government should tighten **its** policies*, with singular *its*? Or do you say *the government should tighten **their** policies*, with plural *their*? You might feel you can imagine both, here. Yet there are instances where singular *its* sounds so ludicrous that a plural rendition is the only possibility. For instance, *the audience is clapping its hands and stamping its feet* sounds plainly daft. So does *an army marching on its stomach* (apologies to Napoleon). The image of a single body just doesn't work. Sometimes you can think of these collectives only in terms of their individual members and not as a single entity. *The audience are clapping their hands and stamping their feet* is the only possibility. Grammar books that insist these collectives are strictly singular, and therefore demand they take a singular verb, are being too simplistic. OK, you might insist that *audience* is singular and you must therefore say *the audience **is** large*, but this would then dictate that you say *the audience is now taking **its** seats*, which is clearly inelegant. To insist upon a singular verb in this case is not only overpendantic, it results in a sentence verging on the absurd. (Mind you, I'm not too sure about that *army marching on their stomachs!*)

There are many other contexts that provoke a similar tug of war between grammar and meaning. For example, a number of expressions are notionally plural but singular in appearance. These include quantifying expressions like *a lot of* and *a number of*. Grammar books suggest you use singular verbs here too. Yet, in meaning they are similar to other quantifying words like *many* and *most*, and a sentence such as *a lot of papers is lying on the ground* sounds truly ghastly – *a lot of papers are lying on the ground* is really the only possibility. It's as if we've reinterpreted *a lot of papers* as *alotta papers*, with *alotta* as a single quantifying expression. Similarly, a phrase like *a couple* could never be singular despite its structure. Correct grammar would require *a couple* to take a singular verb, but how does this sound to you: *I bought six bread rolls, and a couple was stale?* Awful! It has to be *a couple were stale*. English is full of these sorts of mismatches between meaning and the strict rules of grammar – common sense seems to require one thing, yet grammar demands another.

Are/Is twenty chairs sufficient?

There are other kinds of quantity expressions where the grammar is pretty murky. Let's say you're wondering how many chairs to bring to a party. You might ask the question: 'Is twenty chairs sufficient?' With the singular verb *is* you're treating the chairs *en masse* as a bulk amount, in which case you opt for a singular verb. Then again, you might also think of these as twenty individual chairs, in which case you'd probably ask: 'Are twenty chairs sufficient?' with a plural verb. In this instance, either of these sentences is correct. But again, perhaps I should say 'either of these sentences

are correct'. That's a tricky one too. *Either*, like *neither*, takes a singular verb, yet we clearly have more than one object, or sentence, in mind. The matter of agreement, in language as in the real world, is an awkward business.

Less (?!) than twelve items

It must be the frustration of waiting in supermarket queues that triggers such fury in many normally laid-back shoppers when they are confronted with the sign *Twelve items or less*. The fury is undoubtedly fuelled by the many grammatical descriptions that state such usage is straightforwardly wrong. '*Less* is the comparative form of *little*. It refers to bulk not to number', says my *Essential Companion to Written English*. In other words, *less* means 'not as **much**' and goes with mass nouns. For example, when water restrictions are in place, we all should be using **less** water. *Fewer* means 'not as **many**'. It goes with plural nouns that are countable. So when water restrictions are in place, we should also be taking **fewer** baths. It seems straightforward. So why can't the supermarkets get it right?

But language is never a simple matter of putting a tick or cross beside a sentence – it's always much more interesting than that. The history of these two words *fewer* and *less* is a fascinating one, especially when you compare them to their near relative, the quantifying word *more*. Originally, English made a similar distinction for this word too. *More* was used with noncountable nouns or quantities, for example, *more water*. A different form *mo* (or northern English *mae*) was used for plural, countable nouns such as *mo/mae baths*. However, we lost this form sometime during the early Modern English period and *more* came to be used with both countable and noncountable nouns. (It would, anyway, have been difficult to keep *more* and *mo* apart in pronunciation, at least in some dialects.) So these days we all say both *more water* and *more baths*. We don't distinguish bulk from number here. When this happened, not surprisingly, it encouraged *less* to behave in a parallel fashion with both countable and noncountable nouns. *Less water* and *less baths* became usual. In fact, this sort of usage was happening even before that. As early as Old English, *less* was used freely for *fewer*. If they'd had express lanes and supermarkets a thousand years ago, the sign could well have read *Twelve items or less*.

In short, all indications were that *less* was taking over from *fewer* in the same way that *more* took over from *mo*. But, as can happen in language, speakers had a change of heart. Expressions such as *less baths* became stigmatised and, sometime during the 18th century, well and truly fell from grace. The new grammar books of Standard English called for the distinction between *less* and *fewer* to be maintained. Good grammar demanded *less water* and *fewer baths*. Hence the rule we still find preserved today in books such as my *Essential Companion to Written English*.

But the *less–fewer* distinction is hard to maintain, especially when you consider how *more* behaves. And things also get complex when quantities are involved. Take, for example, quantities of time, as in *seven weeks*. It's a plural noun (suggesting it should take *fewer*), but then again it's a single period lasting seven weeks. Hence, even usage commentators suggest that *less* may occur here; for example, *in less than seven weeks I'll be on Cottesloe Beach* actually sounds better than *in fewer than seven weeks I'll be on Cottesloe Beach*. This is also the case with with quantities of money, as in *I've got less than ten dollars*. Why *less* here? Well, in this case, what's being referred to is a single sum of money, '$10'. If you said *fewer than ten dollars*, it'd sound like you're referring to ten single dollar coins.

And now, what about that sign at the supermarket checkout that reads *Express lane: twelve items or less*? The significant point here is that the word *items* is missing from the end of the phrase. So even though we're dealing with something that is clearly countable, the absence of *items* suggests that a quantity is involved. Consider also examples like *tutorials should have twenty students or less* and *classes should have no less than twenty students*. These are examples of countable nouns but they're also being quantified, hence *less* sounds acceptable. In fact, it seems pretty clear that the use of *less* in place of *fewer* in these contexts is on the increase all round the English-speaking world. Even dictionaries now list *fewer* as one of the definitions of *less*.

As is typical of language change, this has produced stylistic differences. In less conservative varieties of English, *less* is behaving like *more* and appears with both countable and noncountable nouns. Since this is the innovative pattern, it sounds more informal to say *less students*. In the more conservative varieties, *less* is still being used like *much* – with noncountable nouns only. So to our ears it sounds more formal to say *fewer students*. But even the more conservative speakers have a hard time maintaining the distinction when the countable nouns are quantified, as in *no fewer than twenty students*. On these occasions most of us are guilty of saying *no less than twenty students*. All the signs indicate that *less* will eventually oust *fewer* and both *more* and *less* will apply equally to nouns of count and measure. This change is hardly surprising – pattern neatening is a strong force in language change, and there is considerable pressure for *less* to behave like *more*. After all, until the 18th century it was doing exactly this.

Dangling modifiers

Not long ago my Head of School alerted me to a statement that appeared in the *Advertising and Community Services Bulletin* of my university. It read: 'On Wednesday, [we] will participate in an International Day of Student Action. At 1pm, a banner will be dropped from the building, followed by three prominent speakers.' Here is one fine example of the dreaded dangling modifier – or detached participle, if you want its more formal label. A phrase like the one here – 'followed by three prominent speakers' – is a mini clause containing the participle *followed*. Such a phrase should be attached to something, but in this example it is left dangling outside, and so produces the hilarious image of a 'day of action' that includes dropping from the building top a banner as well as three prominent speakers.

Crimes of grammar like this one are especially obvious in writing. In speech we're guilty of all sorts of linguistic malpractice that's never picked up by our audience. There's too much happening, and it's all happening far too fast for people to notice the infelicities of style and structure that go whizzing by. But that's the nature of speech – it's fast and furious. Writing is a different kettle of fish. Dangling modifiers such as the one above have a comical effect and are therefore distracting to readers. If something is distracting, then it will interfere with effective communication and even a laid-back linguist like me would say – it deserves to be stomped on!

But this is where I can't help myself. I feel I also have to point out that even the finest examples of written Standard English are full of dangling modifiers that go undetected, even by linguistic health inspectors. This is because their meanings are more abstract. Indeed, many of them are conventionalized sentence builders – phrases such as *regarding, considering, seeing that, provided that, assuming that*. These supply the framework for the rest of the sentence that follows. They're useful expressions for announcing the arrival of a new topic. They're the linguistic equivalent of trumpet blasts or fanfares, and no one ever connects them with the dreaded dangling modifier – which is, after all, precisely what they are.

Passives

I have a new computer. My old one finally gave up the ghost. This new one is a mixed blessing, I have to say. For one thing it comes with a grammar checker. Green squiggly lines now alert me to grammatical errors, infelicities of style, and all those other horrors of my writing. Of course I can turn it off. But the truth is, as irritating as I find them, it is also strangely fascinating to see these green squiggly lines appear (all too frequently) underneath parts of my prose.

Clearly, one of the structures it has in its sights is the poor old passive. Every passive construction I use seems to automatically attract the green squiggle (as do, I should add, plenty of constructions that aren't in fact passive but my checker thinks they are!). Now, I know that the ins and outs of fine grammatical distinctions like active and passive have escaped many people. Many have a vague and often ghastly recollection of such things being taught to them at school. So let me firstly say something about the passive and, more importantly, why it is we have it.

Originally, English word order was much freer than it is today. In Old English, it was information structure that basically determined the position of elements. Flexible word order meant that words could simply move around as required, to get attention and create expectation, for instance. But in the modern language, word order has become more rigid. In basic clauses the subject comes first, then the verb, then everything else. So, how can we continue to accentuate and emphasize crucial parts of our message within the confines of such rigid conventions? While English grammar might require fixed word order, discourse requires word order rearrangements for expressive ends. We've resolved this conflict by evolving a set of special devices that somehow satisfy both conditions. We now have at our disposal a number of what could be called subject-forming strategies. These create new subjects, and this then gives us more flexibility as to what we put in first position in the sentence. The passive is one of these constructions.

Take the sentence *Azog the Goblin killed your Grandfather Thror.* This is the active construction. The passive version reverses this order – *Your Grandfather Thror was killed by Azog the Goblin.* (My grammar checker has just confirmed this.) This is in fact how Tolkien chose to write a sentence in *The Hobbit.* Of course, had there been grammar checkers in his day, he would have copped a green squiggly line, too. You'll notice with the passive version, the meaning remains the same. It's what appears in focal position that's changed. What Tolkien wanted us to focus our attention on was the appallingly wicked *Azog the Goblin.* Hence the passive allows this phrase to appear in the end position, which is where an exciting new revelation should go. Whether the active or passive is used is not a matter of 'grammar'. It depends on the discourse context and factors to do with the information status of the items involved – for example, whether they bring old or new tidings, whether they're assumed or are surprising and unpredictable. In short, there are very good reasons to use the passive.

Another advantage of the passive is that it allows us to omit certain information. This can be very handy when the information is not particularly relevant or perhaps is already blatantly obvious. In fact, most passives that appear in ordinary language are agentless – there's no '*by*' phrase. If we had already been told who had killed Grandfather Thror, for example, Tolkien could well have rendered this sentence simply as 'Your Grandfather Thror was killed'. The following is an extract from a piece that appeared in the magazine *Vogue Entertaining*. It's chock-a-block with agentless passives.

> *At Armstrong's Tables of Toowong fat oysters had been lifted from their shells, and then returned onto a gently spiced cushion of noodles, touched with an olive oil, lemon and saltwater vinaigrette, and topped with a dollop of oscietra caviar. Linguini had been tossed in truffle oil, studded with shards of crisp asparagus, topped with a soft-poached egg and a generous slice of fresh, black truffle.*

Sounds gorgeous – and it's beautifully written too. Yet every clause is a passive. We can take for granted that it's the chefs who are doing all this lifting, returning, touching, topping, tossing and studding. Here the passive allows the writer to omit unexciting information that would otherwise have to be stated in the active version. Why bother to say *The chefs had tossed the linguini in truffle oil* when *Linguini had been tossed in truffle oil* is much more effective?

OK, of course there's scope for misuse here. Doing away with agents can be useful when it's precisely desirable to conceal information. For example, on some occasions it'd be very honest of me to say *I ate the chocolate*. More likely I'd resort to the passive, to down-play my involvement. A sneakier way of putting it would be *the chocolate has been eaten*. The small child who says *the window got broken* has already learnt the value of agentless passives! These constructions are also characteristic of the impersonal (and some would argue pretentious) style found in a lot of academic writing – and of course in bureaucratic writing, too. With the right vocabulary, passives can make even the most simple and mundane topics sound complex and profound: *the requisite accommodation for stationary vehicles has been provided* – so the council are giving us parking spots!

It's this sort of inappropriate use of the passive that has given the construction a bad name. Not surprisingly, it has become the *bête noire* of many Plain English translators, who see it as a source of confusion for readers. But the problem has been overstated and the behaviour of our computer grammar checkers is quite harebrained – most of those green squiggles are unwarranted.

There is/there are grave fears

An ABC listener, Arthur of Evatt in Canberra, posed an interesting question concerning sentences such as *There is still grave fears*. Certainly traditional English grammar would argue that the plural phrase *grave fears* is the subject. Therefore the verb should also be plural, and *There are grave fears* is the correct version. So why do some speakers of current English appear to be violating a fundamental rule of grammar? Why are they saying, and indeed writing, things like *There is still grave fears*?

'Language will change, and has to change', Arthur of Evatt writes. 'It's not the change but the "Why" of the change that I cannot always fathom.' It's a good point, and to understand what's going on here we need to go back a fair way in English language history.

When English word order became less flexible, we lost the handy ability to simply move elements around in the sentence. As I have earlier described, in compensation for this the language evolved special constructions such as the passive, so that we could continue to shift elements around but within the confines of our stricter word order. At the same time that English was developing its passive construction, it was also evolving elements that you might think of as empty subjects: words like *it* and *there*. These are meaningless little words that simply appear in the place of the subject and allow us to delay the appearance of other elements until later in the sentence. Hence, they're often called 'dummy' subjects. Tolkien, for example, could have chosen to begin his tale about Bilbo Baggins this way: *A hobbit lived in a hole in the ground*. But he did it much more effectively by using the dummy subject *there*: *In a hole in the ground **there** lived a hobbit*. The hobbit is new exciting information, and for that reason is better placed late in the sentence – it's old, dull, familiar background information that belongs at the beginning. So the word *there* in a sense holds the place of the subject, to allow the surprising phrase *a hobbit* to appear later. The reader first imagines a hole in the ground and then – surprise! – a hobbit; not, say, a rabbit.

A brief aside

Here, I want to interrupt and quickly point out something interesting about *there is* versus *there are*. It has to do with the question of verb agreement. Even Standard English allows a curious exception, as shown by this wonderful example I once came upon in a magazine: *There is a long-legged dominatrix, a nun in vinyl, a gum-chewing school-girl, an inflatable doll, a double D fat-o-gram wench and Edwina scissor hands.* There's much that is striking about this sentence, granted, but let us focus on the verb *is*. It has to be singular, even though what follows it is clearly plural. Put the sentence another way and you can see this more clearly: *A long-legged dominatrix, a nun in vinyl, a gum-chewing school-girl, an inflatable doll, a double D fat-o-gram wench and Edwina scissor hands* **are** here. But when *There* heads the sentence, the verb suddenly becomes singular: *There **is** a long-legged dominatrix and a nun in vinyl.* It's the word *there* that's triggering the singular verb. If *There is grave fears* is a violation of the rules of English grammar, then surely this is too?

So, back to Arthur of Evatt's *There are grave fears.* What I'd argue here is that traditional grammar is in fact wrong in assuming *grave fears* to be the grammatical subject. Now, before you skip this page in disgust, let me point out some of the features of grammatical subjects in English. For a start, if you form a question in English, it's always the subject and the first verb that swap places. Look what happens when we form a question from *There are grave fears – Are there grave fears?* It's *there* and *are* that swap places. English also has a handful of words that distinguish subjects from objects. These are pronouns such as *I* versus *me*, *he* versus *him*. I could ask the question *Who's coming to the party?* You might reply *Well, there's me.* It's the word *me* that's interesting here. This is the form of the object. So what's the subject? It must be *there*.

I can keep applying similar tests. Each time they'll suggest the same thing. *There* is the structural subject in sentences like *there are grave fears*. Sure, it's not a typical subject, but it is behaving like one. There are clearly good grammatical grounds for assuming this. Or should I say, there **is** good grammatical grounds? – for this looks to be the construction of the future.

Computer mouses?

In a recent issue of *Ozwords* (a magazine of the Australian Dictionary Centre), P James from Western Australia posed an interesting question. It concerned the plural of the computer mouse – 'is it *mice* or *mouses?*' asked P James. 'I have heard both. But *mouses* sounds very odd.' The editor rightly pointed out that during the 18th century people began to use the word *mouse* in various technical senses when referring to items that somehow resembled a mouse. The nautical mouse was a pear-shaped knob on the outside of a knot. The plumber's mouse was a small weight with a cord attached. Yet another mouse was a match used for firing guns. The plural for all these technical 'mice' was often *mouses*. The computer mouse grew out of this tradition and dates from around the mid-1960s. What I want to look at now is the process that turns *mice* into *mouses* and, more particularly, why *computer mouses*, or *tailor's gooses* for that matter, are reasonable English, whereas *mouses* and *gooses* in ordinary usage are generally not. Why is this so?

There's fairies at the bottom of my garden

In speech it is much more usual to hear *there's* (as in *there's still grave fears*) rather than the full form *there is*. Even in writing, I often use this contracted form. In a sense it's become a kind of introductory particle, akin to *how's* as in *how's things?* or even *let's* as in *let's go!* (usually pronounced 'sgo'). Probably we should stop including the apostrophe here and think of these items as forms that have fused to become single units.

These expressions are doing precisely what many of our little grammatical words have done. Take the word *while*, for example. It grew out of the Old English phrase *þa hwile þe*, literally, 'during the while [a period of time] that'. Similarly, the conjoining word *but* developed from the location expression *be-utan*: literally, 'on the outside'. Time works as a kind of compressing agent. The expressions grow shorter. You'll notice, too, that the meanings become more abstract. *There's* in *there's fairies at the bottom of my garden* would have grown out of a location expression. An example would be *Look!* **There's** *a fairy!* where *there's* is quite literally pointing to the fairy. The spoken phrase *there's* in this instance has a longer vowel and a more concrete sense of location or position. Only a hint of this meaning lingers on in a sentence such as *There's fairies at the bottom of my garden*.

The process that changes *mice* to *mouses* is called analogy and it's undoubtedly one of the most important forces behind language change. Basically, analogy takes a form of a language and changes it to become more like some other form with which it is associated. So *cheese* is to *cheeses* as *mouse* is to *mouses*. The linguist Jean Aitchison once described it as a kind of 'tidying up process' and you can see why. The regular way we form plurals in English today is with the ending -*s*, and the task of analogy is to take any irregular forms and whip them into line. For example, *eyen* has now become *eyes* and *handa* has become *hands*. So, if analogy has been cleaning up the language in this way, why has it failed with irregular plurals like *mice, geese, feet, teeth* and *men*?

It's the everyday nature of this vocabulary that has preserved these forms. Words like *mice* and *men* are very frequently used words. Children acquire them early, and through repetition, it seems, they become so entrenched in the memory that they're fortified against changes occurring elsewhere. Frequently used irregular nouns appear to be stored individually in the brain, and are protected in that way. As the American linguist Joan Bybee describes it, the more we access them, the more they dig in and are able to resist the regularizing forces outside. I've mentioned this before. It's always the high-frequency words that are the badly behaved ones when it comes to grammar, precisely because they are so successful at resisting the cleaning-up activities of analogy. Novel uses such as the technical *mouses* and *gooses* have taken *mice* and *geese* outside of their everyday domain, and this has given analogy the opportunity to step in and regularize them.

There's another factor that probably helps analogy to clean up irregular terms. Often they are hidden inside what look like compound words, and when analogy is on a regularizing binge, compounds usually fall in line. For instance, none of you would be tempted to use the plural *foots* or *tooths*, yet *pinkfoots* (a kind of

Frequency and grammar change

 We can also see the conservative effects of frequency on grammatical sequences. Some time back I did a study of the changes that have taken place in marking negatives in English and its relatives Dutch and German. What was striking in all these languages was the way common usage verbs like *think* and *know* clung to older patterns of negation. For example, in the course of Early Modern English we acquired a rule called *do*-support. No longer was it acceptable to say something like *I read not*. Negative sentences had to be formed with *do*: in other words, *I do not read.* This rule came into force during the 18th century. Even so, for a very long time common usage verbs like *speak, think* and *know* preserved the earlier, simpler pattern. They formed the negative with *not* only, as in *I speak not, I think not, I know not.* It seems that these verbs in combination with *not* were stored in the memory as individual chunks or units, much like idioms. Their frequency of use meant speakers accessed them easily and they were strong enough to resist the changes that were affecting all the other verbs in the language.

flamingo) and *sabertooths* (a kind of tiger) sound OK. These words have to be compounds – hence *pinkfoots have pink feet* (at least I assume they do; to be honest I've never seen a pinkfoot). So it's really only the basic forms like *feet* and *teeth* that can resist analogy. The derived forms like *pinkfoots* and *sabertooths* conform and behave like all other nouns. They are subject to the regular rule of plural formation. So, back to the mouse that belongs with our computers. Its plural *mouses* probably came about via the compound *computer mouse*. Somehow the form *mouses* isn't quite so jarring when it occurs in the full expression *computer mouses* – in the same way that the *foots*, the *leafs*, the *mouses* and the *gooses* don't stand out in *goosefoots* (a type of plant), *Maple Leafs* (the famous Canadian ice hockey team), *Mickey Mouses* (university courses for students who want an easy time of it) and *tailor's gooses* (irons used in tailoring, so called because of their goose-shaped necks).

Finally, there's one other curious aspect to the workings of analogy. Typically, when a new analogical formation is accepted, it takes on the primary function of the word, and the older irregular form, if it remains in use at all, is restricted to second-ary and more specialist functions – it could be in religious, poetic or technical spheres. For example, *brethren*, the older plural for *brother*, is now restricted to religious usage. *Brothers* is the form we find in everyday language. Similarly, the normal plural of *cow* these days is of course *cows*. Yet the older plural *kine* lingers on as a poetic term. 'When the kine have given a pailful' is a line I recall from a folk song – *kine* sounds more romantic than *cows*.

It's not just nouns that behave this way. Originally, the com-parative of the adjective *old* was *elder*, but on analogy of forms like *bold–bolder* we now have *old–older*. *Elder* today has limited usage in special expressions such as *elder statesman* and *elders of the church*. In technical contexts the old adjective form *molten* con-tinues to be used for substances that require a great deal of heat to melt them, as in *molten lead*. Yet it's certainly *melted* cheese that appears on top of our everyday cheese on toast or cauliflower casserole – none of you, I trust, would be tempted by molten cheese on toast.

The earmarks of jargon

 The debris left by language change often turns into the conservative idiosyncrasies of jargons. It seems that the specialized content of a jargon encourages a more rigid style that then acts as a kind of embalming fluid. These items become a matter of stylistic choice: conventionalised earmarks of the variety. Think of the *witnesseths, thereons, hereinafters* and *herebefores* that have lingered in legal language long after they've been ousted by ordinary speakers. Even archaic word order patterns (*What say you?*) become bits of grammatical routine and are bound up with the ritual magic of the legal process. This works for meanings too. Think of the legal *instrument*, meaning 'formal document'. This very old usage dates back to at least the 15th century. But I shouldn't always poke fun at legal jargon. My own jargon is full of fossils. Most jargons are. I've just recently learnt that some pastry chefs still talk about *coffins* for pastry cases. This specialist culinary sense stems directly from the original meaning of the word *coffin* for any kind of case or box. Cook-speak, you'll find, abounds in delightful archaisms.

Never say die

Some time back on HISTLING (the Internet discussion group for historical linguists), linguist Larry Trask posed an interesting question. It had to do with the loss of the word *die* as the singular of the word *dice*. He wrote: 'Traditionally, a spotted cube used in playing certain games is called a "die", with the uniquely irregular plural "dice". This is still, I think, the position in American English. In British English, however, the singular "die" has almost wholly disappeared, and the singular form is now "dice".' Replies came from all over the English-speaking world and showed up some fascinating differences.

101

The responses fell into three main groups. One lot of speakers had simply never heard of the singular noun *die*, unless it referred to a 'metal stamp used for coining'. For them, *dice* was the only form for 'a small cube with six spotted faces', and it was used for both singular and plural. A second group had heard of singular *die*, but found it a fussy and pretentious form that they had only ever encountered in grammar books. The last group found singular *die* a perfectly respectable alternative to singular *dice*, but less usual. It would seem that Larry Trask was correct – 'users of "die" are a dying breed'. I should add that Larry Trask himself was an habitual user of *die* in the singular. He would then fall into a fourth and minor group – a group of 'tedious old farts' was how he described them.

So it would seem that singular *die* is definitely on its last legs, probably best preserved in American English. American board games apparently continue to instruct the players to 'throw a die'. In fact, American dictionaries list only **singular** *die* and don't recognise singular *dice*. Certainly, board games in Australia would instruct players to 'throw a dice' and I gather it's the same in the UK. It is surprising, then, that both my *Oxford* and *Macquarie* dictionaries give clear preference to the older singular *die* and not *dice*, although they do point out that *dice* is often construed as singular. Clearly our dictionaries are asleep at the switch here – both in Australia and the UK singular *dice* is the norm.

In fact, there are signs that in Australia the situation is becoming more complicated still. Prompted by Larry Trask's query, Alan Dench from the University of Western Australia took a straw poll of colleagues up and down his corridor and all agreed that yes, certainly *dice* is the singular form, but *die* is its plural! So this is a different outcome again. In this case, speakers are reinterpeting *die* as a plural form, perhaps on the pattern of highfalutin plurals like *octopi* and *platypi*. I don't think this is just a West Australian phenomenon by any means. I've certainly encountered speakers from other parts of Australia who (if they know the term *die*) also construe it as the plural of *dice*.

For most speakers around the English-speaking world, *dice* is singular and also plural, although some have created a new plural *dices*. Clearly, the word *dice* is going the same way as *pence*, originally the collective plural of the word *penny*. Of course, no one worries these days over (historically anomalous) expressions like *one pence* – or for that matter *twopences* and *threepences* which, strictly speaking, are doubly marked plurals. The original plural ending of both words *pence* and *dice* has been misconstrued as part of the stem. This process occurs more readily where the plural is unusual. In *dice* and *pence* the ending is voiceless, which is odd. It's as if speakers don't feel the ending to be plural enough, so they reinterpret the word as singular. There are plenty of examples of this. The word *bodice* was originally the plural of *body; chintz* derives from plural of *chint* 'a painted calico from India'. (Chintz no longer looks plural because it's been given a fancy respelling with a 'z'.) The words *quince* and *lettuce* both come from French plural words. Just like the others, they now have a new plural form *quinces* and *lettuces*.

So it's unlikely that singular *die* will endure. Even in North America there are strong signs that *dice* is winning out as the singular. Of course, we still continue to use expressions like *the die is cast*, but then perhaps you're like me – I certainly never connected this expression with the small spotted cube. It was only when I checked the dictionary that I realized it had to do with throwing dice. I think I'd always assumed that it referred to metal casting. Well, it makes sense! After all, the expression does mean 'a decisive step has been taken'. So the idea of pouring metal into a mould is also quite appropriate. In fact, I didn't realize either that *straight as a die*, meaning 'honest or loyal', had to do with throwing dice as well. It's amazing what you can learn from the dictionary. But my favourite dictionary entry for *die* and *dice* is that written by Ambrose Bierce in his *Devil's Dictionary* of 1911. It reads '*Die* noun. The singular of "dice". We seldom hear the word, because there is a prohibitory proverb "Never say die".'

Reconstructing the past

Linguistic curiosities in modern-day language are often the result of historical developments. Take word order. As mentioned earlier, Old English from a thousand years ago showed considerably more flexibility than Modern English. All logically possible arrangements of subject, verb and object appeared during that time, although the verb usually appeared at the end of a sentence, unless there was a good reason for putting it somewhere else. Since then, the language has seen a gradual shift towards the verb-second word order we find in Modern English. The verb now usually appears after its subject and before its object. But there are interesting relics of the earlier verb-final word order. Take, for example, words such as *bloodshed, roll call, self-pity, woodcut, leasehold*, or *babysit*. These are noun–verb compounds that involve verbs in combination with their objects; in other words, you shed blood (*bloodshed*); you call the roll (*roll call*); you pity yourself (*self-pity*). What you'll notice here is that the ordering is always the object followed by the verb, so even though you *shed blood* the compound is *bloodshed*. Examples of the reverse order (namely, verb+object), such as *pickpocket* and *pastime*, are rare. The vast majority of our modern-day compounds show the unusual object+verb order – they're linguistic leftovers from the earlier verb-final nature of English.

You can find lots of these fossils in our present-day grammar. Modern pronouns are a good example – those odd forms like *I* versus *me* and *my; he* versus *him* and *his; who* versus *whom* and *whose*. These are also grammatical remnants, this time of an earlier system involving what are known as inflections – grammatical endings, that signal the relationships between words in a sentence. Due to enormous changes that have taken place, English now signals this grammatical information in different ways. For example, in *The queen loved the king* versus *The king loved the queen*, it's now the order which tells us who is loving who (or should that be whom?). The endings that would have once told us this are now gone.

Of course, in the case of English, we have old documents going back around a thousand years, and so we know about earlier grammatical patterns. But usually we're not this lucky. For most of the languages of the world, there is no written evidence available and we have to go on any such fossil material we can find. By sifting through this rubble we might be lucky enough to uncover clues to reconstruct something of the prehistory of these languages.

An/a history?

A question I'm frequently asked is whether it is more correct to say *a history* or *an history*. Is it *a hotel* or *an hotel*? Both *a* and *an* are called indefinite articles and the general rule for their use – on the surface at least – is quite straightforward. It's a pronunciation thing, and has to do with the sounds that follow. If the word following begins with a consonant, then the form is *a* (as in *a sandwich*), and if it begins with a vowel then it's *an* (as in *an open sandwich*). As a little historical aside – both forms *a* and *an* developed late in English. They grew out of the word for the numeral *one* – it's a very typical development. Hence, the shape of *an*. It preserves the original 'n' of the number *one*.

This alternating pattern *a/an* is exactly what we find with the spoken version of the so-called 'definite article' *the*. It's just less obvious here because the different forms are not reflected in the spelling. What's involved is a more subtle change that has to do with the pronunciation of the vowel sound. Basically, when *the* appears before words beginning with consonants (as in *the sandwich*), it has a shorter more relaxed little vowel than *the* before words beginning with vowels (as in *the open sandwich*). In the second version, the vowel is a more substantial sound (pronounced something like 'thee').

It's always sounds that condition these changes to *a* or *the*, not written letters. Spelling is not involved here. So even though we write a word such as *useful* with an initial vowel, in pronunciation it actually begins with a consonant sound 'y'. Hence, *a useful sandwich* and not *an useful sandwich*. Conversely, there are some initial consonants in spelling that are never pronounced: for example the 'h' in words such as *honour* or *hour*. Hence, *an honour* and not *a honour*.

So far so good. But this is language, of course, and we expect wrinkles. One wrinkle has to do with the pronunciation of 'h'. It's a weakly articulated sound and is prone to disappearance acts. Even though many of you would never admit to dropping your aitches, you'll probably find in fact that when 'h' appears at the beginning of an unstressed syllable, especially in normal rapid speech, it's only natural for you to delete it. So, even though you wouldn't say *an habit* or *an hero*, it seems quite acceptable to say *an habitual action* or *an heroic effort*. Because the 'h' is virtually inaudible in both *habitual* and *heroic*, at least when they occur in a string of words such as *an habitual action*, we treat these words as if they began with a vowel sound. You might have noticed examples in this book such as *an historical event* and *an habitual user*. Since the 'h' is also barely audible here, I prefer these versions to *a historical event* and *a habitual user*, which seem to me to be very inelegant. Besides, *an historical event* and *an habitual user* have a classier ring to them!

There's an interesting historical aspect to all this. At one time it was considered quite OK to drop the aitch. This is why in conservative texts like the King James Bible you still find *an* before many nouns beginning with 'h', even where the aitch occurs in stressed syllables as in *an hundred* or *an harlot*. It's surprising, in fact, that aitch didn't disappear entirely from our sound system. Up until the mid-1700s, deleting aitch didn't raise an eyebrow – even linguistic fusspots of the time could be heard dropping their aitches. But there was then one of those curious social reversals you sometimes find in language change. Aitch-dropping suddenly became a bad thing, and since the 1800s there has been considerable social pressure to hang onto the sound. It's curious, then, that something like *an historical event* sounds slightly more posh to us than *a historical event*, even though it has the dreaded dropped aitch. Presumably its poshness stems from early times before aitch-dropping was stigmatized.

I should point out that when the aitch was restored sometime during the 1800s, false aitches were occasionally added. Words like *hotel*, *hospital* and *herb* were borrowed from French, and when we borrowed them they would have been aitchless. The modern American usage that doesn't pronounce the aitch in *herb*, and occasionally also *hotel*, stems from this time – *an herb* and *an hotel* is historically accurate. But when English aitch-dropping fell from grace, people went overboard and started restoring the sound even to French words where it didn't belong.

Let me mention another final hiccup in this complex story of *a* versus *an*. We're dealing here with an aspect of English grammar that's currently on the move. You might have observed this change already in younger speakers. I mentioned at the start that the general rule puts reduced *a* and also *the* before words beginning

He only died yesterday

There is a very large sign outside a coat shop close to where I live. It reads *We only sell coats*. Now, I pondered long and hard on the word *only* when I first encountered this sign. Does this mean they sell only coats – which isn't strictly true, because they also sell other clothing items. So perhaps it **does** really mean they *only* sell them; they won't buy them back. In speech, ambiguity like this would never arise. The nature of speech means that speakers have a whole support system of oral and visual cues that are not available to writers. Features such as intonation, pitch and loudness indicate the focus of the word *only*, and the immediate context would too.

Small modifying words such as *only* often appear to be in the wrong place. One reason for this is that they tend to seek out the company of verbs. As the core of the sentence, the verb acts as a kind of magnet here, hence curiosities like *he only died yesterday*, where what's intended, of course, is *he died only yesterday*. In writing, with no prosodic prompts, the placement of *only* is more crucial. Its meaning will be taken to extend over what follows it. So a misplaced *only* that's attracted to the verb will often stand out and be distracting. Perhaps this was the intention of *We only sell coats*. After all, the aim of an advertising billboard is to draw attention to itself, and 'sloppy' grammar is one effective way. If it hadn't been for its misplaced *only*, I likely would have walked right past this particular advertisement.

with consonants, and puts *an* and a longer *the* ('thee') before words beginning with vowels. But more and more we hear the short forms of these two words before words beginning with **both** consonants **and** vowels, so *a open sandwich*, for example. This development is not unexpected. The general trend for short grammatical words like *a* and *the* is that they become even shorter, until eventually they can no longer stand by themselves and end up as endings or prefixes on other words. These forms *a/an* and also *the* will probably become prefixes too – but that is a whole 'nother' story!

'The Wife's Tale of Bath'

There is much that is interesting about the history of possessive marking in English. And here I'm not talking about apostrophes, but the development of the actual *-s* ending that we find today in expressions like *the boy's photo*. It is a relic from Old English, when possession was signalled by a whole host of different endings that could appear on nouns. These endings have since disappeared. But the *-s* ending was clearly a survivor and a thousand years later it's still hanging in there, although its nature has changed remarkably.

Originally, the 's' was a word ending. It would attach itself only to the word that indicated the actual possessor itself. Take, for instance, *The Wife of Bath's Tale*. In Modern English the *Wife of Bath* is felt to be one unit, and the *-s* ending attaches itself at the end of this unit, hence *The Wife of Bath's Tale*. But when Chaucer wrote his Canterbury Tales he didn't express it this way, but rather *The Wife's Tale of Bath*. Here you can see that the phrase *Wife of Bath* is split into two – and the *-s* is attached to the end of *Wife*. During the early Modern English period both types of construction were available – for example, *the King's galleons of Spain* versus the more familiar *the King of Spain's galleons*.

This is typical of language change. Takeovers aren't instant and neat. Expressions that are on the way out will exist side-by-side with the new arrivals, often for some time. Usually there are stylistic differences. The newer expression will sound less formal and often, of course, raise a few eyebrows. Meanwhile the older expression will sound increasingly fusty until it finally disappears. This is what has happened here. In the course of the 16th century it became no longer possible to say something like *the King's galleons of Spain* or *The Wife's Tale of Bath* and mean the same thing.

At first blush this mightn't seem such a remarkable development – but it is. An ending on a noun normally remains a word ending and doesn't detach itself in this way. In Modern English you might even say something like *that chap over there in the corner's wife*. OK, it's colloquial and you probably wouldn't write it, but these sorts of examples are rife in speech. In fact, you can find extraordinary instances where the *-s* appears right at the end of extremely long and complex phrases. The most remarkable example I've ever encountered comes from a colleague of mine, JC Smith from Oxford. Here's the gem he overheard in his college common room – *this guy who I used to know at school and who went to Cambridge and got a first in engineering's brother*. It is of course *the guy's brother!*

So what is the future of possessive marking in English? Well, as linguists will always point out, predicting language change is a dicey business. Perhaps the *-s* ending will eventually go the way of all other endings and disappear, supplanted by the *of* construction as in *the brother of the guy*. It was during the Middle Ages that the word *of* made its move and started encroaching on the territory of the *-s* ending. During the 16th and 17th centuries the situation was very much as you find it today – the *-s* ending was favoured with human nouns (for example, *the boy's book*) and the *of* construction more popular with inanimate nouns (*the cover of the book*). But the popularity of *of* is increasing. It's now also commonly heard where human nouns are involved, as in *the release of the prisoner*. It's conceivable that eventually *of* will totally displace the *-s* ending. Certainly, a striking theme running through the story of English is the erosion of this kind of grammatical ending. The possessive ending belongs to a tiny group of seven survivors. All may well disappear with time. More than likely, phrases like *the release of the prisoner* will eventually oust *the prisoner's release*. More than likely, also, the phrase *more tasty* will evict *tastier*, just as *more horrid* evicted *horrider*. You can see that the trend is for endings to be replaced by independent words like *of, more* and *most*. There is one big advantage to losing the *-s* ending. You also avoid the tricky business of when and where to put the apostrophe, something that has plagued English since the 16th century. We've never entirely got it right. Get rid of *-s* and we also get rid of this pesky piece of imported French punctuation.

Horrid redundancy?

 English has a construction that looks to be a doubly marked possessive. For example, *a friend of Mary's* shows possession marked with both the preposition *of* and the ending *-s*. This is a blended construction involving the two ways English has of expressing possession. The use of combinations of words that somehow overlap or copy each other in meaning is guaranteed to cause steam to come out of some ears! Strangely, however, this construction attracts little condemnation these days. Nonetheless, I have a philosophy colleague who finds it an unwarranted grammatical extravagence and extremely irritating. It is to him that I dedicate this box.

In fact, it's not clear that this is a case of wanton extravagence. If I say, for example, *Mary's picture* with the usual possessive *-s* ending on *Mary*, this could mean all sorts of things – a picture that's owned by Mary, painted by Mary, or perhaps a representation of her. It's ambiguous. *A picture of Mary*, on the other hand, can only mean a representation of her. Contrast this with *a picture of Mary's* with double possession. This means a picture painted by Mary or one that is owned by her. *A student of Chomsky's* – double possession again – means a student that studies under Chomsky. *A student of Chomsky* means a student who studies Chomsky or who studies his work. It looks as if speakers are assigning different meanings to these constructions. To say you're *a friend of Greg's* means that Greg looks upon you as a friend. To say you're *a friend of Greg* means that you look upon Greg as a friend. A subtle difference. It seems that the addition of *-s* to Mary, Chomsky or Greg is a way of focusing attention on these people as having a more active role in the relationship being expressed. Double possession has given us a way to express quite fine distinctions that we couldn't convey before. The extra marking is not overkill in this case. But then, you'll find it rarely is.

Gotten – a 'weed in the garden of our verbs'?

I'm not sure what it is about the word *gotten*, but it seems to be a verb form that manages to get up almost everybody's nose, outside of North America, that is. Ordinary laid-back Australians regularly vent spleen on examples such as *It's gotten more spectacular.* So why has *gotten* become such a linguistic atrocity for some speakers? After all, no one bats an eyelid about the related form *forgotten*. And what about those *ill-gotten gains*? No batted eyelids, and yet it contains precisely the same verb form.

One problem for the form *gotten* is that it's become one of the most distinctive features of American English. 'The ugliest Americanism' is how one irate reader of the *Canberra Times* describes it. Already worried that their beloved Aussie lingo has become overrun with slang expressions from the States, it probably seems the last straw for some speakers that we appear to be taking on American grammatical forms as well. And it does look to be gaining ground. Certainly *The Macquarie Dictionary* describes it as on the rise in Australian English, especially in speech.

The verb form *gotten* is another of the many conservative features of American English. It's well-attested from the Middle Ages, but didn't happen to survive in Standard British English and therefore didn't make it into mainstream Australian English. The very first edition of *The Oxford English Dictionary* announced in 1899 that the form *gotten* was as good as dead, except in some dialects. It certainly didn't die out in varieties of Scots. Its resurgence in Australia is usually attributed to American English influence, but it's likely, too, that we've always had vestiges of these dialectal *gotten* users. Perhaps speakers would feel a little less grumpy about *gotten* if they thought of it as the return of a quaint dialectal archaism.

But I wonder, too, whether the dislike of *gotten* also stems from a general loathing of the verb *get*. Various grammatical handbooks still describe *get* as some kind of noxious weed and I'm grateful to my colleagues Heather Bowe and Cindy Allan for drawing my attention to that lovely (and apt) description – '*Get* is a weed in the garden of our verbs'. I certainly remember the weed-removal wars waged on *get* in my school days. I was never quite sure why, but I certainly joined in with the best of them and made sure the verb never appeared in my writing. In *Australian Style*, editor Pam Peters describes the extraordinary lengths some teachers went to in removing all traces of *get* – even to the point of writing the word on a piece of paper and then laying it to rest somewhere in the school grounds. None of these methods worked of course. *Get* continues to be one of the most successful of all verbs. It's such a versatile word, covering a range of different meanings – 'to become, to obtain, to possess, to receive, to buy, to take, to fetch, to arrive, to move'. These are just some of the uses of *get*. It's also a kind of all-purpose auxiliary verb, used in grammar to indicate the passive, as in *He got arrested*; causative *I got him to do it*; and, in conjunction with *have*, as an alternative to *must* or *ought to*, as in *I've got to see him*. Probably the versatility of *get* meant it simply drew too much attention to itself and consequently fell foul of the verbal hygienists. I agree, there are stylistically more exciting verbs to be used, but to banish the verb *get* altogether does seem a little over the top.

But back to its past form *gotten*. Probably what many non-Americans don't realize is that American English speakers use *got* as well as *gotten*, and they employ both in different contexts. (Of course, there's enormous variation in American English – what I'm describing here is what you might think of as General American.) For instance, these speakers won't use *gotten* when *get* has the sense of possession, as in *he's got a new car*. In this context, like Australian and British English speakers, they use simple *got*. American English speakers also won't use *gotten* where the sense is obligation as in *he's got to go*. This allows these speakers to save the *got–gotten* distinction for contexts where there is potential ambiguity. For example in my variety of English, *he's got a new car* can mean 'he possesses a new car' or 'he's acquired a new car'. In American English the sense of acquiring would be expressed by *gotten*, as in *he's gotten a new car* – while *he's got a new car* could only mean therefore 'he possesses a new car'. The *got–gotten* distinction can also be used to distinguish between *I've got to go* meaning 'I must go' and *I've gotten to go* meaning 'I managed to go'. So speakers who use *gotten* are often able to capture finer distinctions than the rest of us.

On the basis of pure linguistics, it's difficult to understand why people should be so hostile towards this verb form. *Gotten* has a lot going for it. But, of course, it's not a matter of linguistics.

People's reactions to *gotten* have deep social underpinnings. America's clout as a cultural superpower makes us Australians feel linguistically insecure, and to many people the use of *gotten* probably seems like letting down our defences.

Got – a horrid neologism

In 1762 there appeared what was arguably the first proper grammar of the English language – the *Short Introduction to English Grammar* written by Bishop Robert Lowth. This was very clear in its recommendations. It outlined that English verbs such as *do*, *write* and *get* should have three distinct forms – *do, did, done*; *write, wrote, written*; and, yes *get, got, **gotten***. Lowth himself provided lists of what he described as common mistakes – committed even by 'some our best Writers', as he described them. Let me quote directly from his grammar:

Thus it is said, He begun, for he began; he run, for he ran; he drunk, for he drank: The Participle being used instead of the Past Time. And much more frequently the Past Time instead of the Participle: as, I had wrote, it was wrote, for I had written, it was written; I have drank, for I have drunk; bore, for born; chose, for chosen; bid, for bidden; got for gotten. This abuse has been long growing upon us, and is continually making further incroachments.

It's interesting to note that one of the 'growing abuses' Lowth highlights is the use of *got* instead of *gotten*. In other words, *gotten* – the word condemned by so many today – is the verb form that carried the stamp of approval in the 1700s.

I should also point out that in his private correspondence, Robert Lowth constantly flouted his own grammatical rule. In a letter to his wife he states, 'My Last was wrote in a great hurry', and later writes in the same letter, 'whose faces and names I have forgot'. (I am grateful to Tieken-Boon van Ostade for alerting me to this.) Perhaps the standard forms he recommended were simply too formal for intimate correspondence. It is hard to know what motivated Lowth's choice here.

He probably wasn't even conscious of the contradiction. As I mentioned at the start of this book, prescriptive endeavours necessarily promote a kind of linguistic doublethink. Language just won't be forced into nice neat compartments labelled 'right' and 'wrong' and anyone who tries to do so will eventually impale themselves on their own prescriptions. Since the beginning of the medieval period, speakers have 'confused' forms such as *wrote* and *written* and *did* and *done*. The different versions continue today and the variation still gives off clear social signals.

May versus might

I regularly receive queries concerning the distinction between *may* and *might*. What worries a lot of people, it seems, is the use of *may* in contexts where *might* seems more appropriate. For example, *He may have seen them* or *Had they the equipment, they may have survived*. The objection made is that there is a wrong sequence of tenses here. Prescriptive grammarians are quite clear on the matter. As Harry Blamires puts it in his *Essential Companion to Written English*, '"May" goes with present and future, "might" with past'. But this only works if you understand *may–might* to have a relationship of present–past. Though this was once the case, it's no longer so straightforward. These verbs have undergone a number of quite complex changes: changes, I should add, that have also taken place in close linguistic relatives such as German.

Here's a bit of a potted history that might help to explain the current confusion of *may* and *might*. Around a thousand years ago *may* had the meaning 'to be able to do something, to have the physical power to do it'. An example from Old English would be *He mæg ridan* ('he has the physical strength to ride'). This sense is preserved in the noun *might*, as in *with all his might*, but has otherwise disappeared. In the course of the 17th century the verb shifted completely from this ability sense to a permitting sense, as in *You may leave now*. In fact, as early as the 14th century *may* had already become the principal verb for expressing permission. In most varieties of English *may* has now yielded this permission sense over to *can* and has sprouted a new meaning, this time 'possibility'. In a sentence such as *It may be ok, I don't know*, the verb *may* has the meaning 'it's possible that'. Occasionally, the sense is ambiguous between permission or possibility, although the possibility sense is now much stronger. In the statement *They may leave tomorrow*, you really only get the permission sense, if the speaker is in some sort of elevated position.

So where does *might* fit in here? Well, *might* was once the past tense of *may*, but it's been asserting its independence since Old English times. It's now really a verb in its own right with its very own meaning. Only vestiges remain of its use as a past form. So when people worry about the inappropriateness of *may* in past contexts, their concerns are ill-founded – quite simply, *may* and *might* have parted company. Of course, the fact that the forms *may* and *might* are unusual has helped this split. By their appearance it's hard for us to think of the relationship between *may* and *might* as being the same as between, say, *sing* and *sang* or *jump* and *jumped*. The present–past relationship is no longer so obvious – *might* simply doesn't look anything like the past of *may*. These sorts of splits in verbs are quite common, especially if the verbs are weird-looking. (Just look at the verb *ought*. This was the original past tense of the verb *owe*. *Owe* has also grown another verb – *own*. So this one verb has split three ways – *owe*, *ought* and *own*.)

But back to *might*. Like *may*, *might* originally had the concrete sense of having the physical power to do something. So when it was the past of *may*, it meant 'had the physical power to'. But this sense disappeared, along with the past permission sense. It no longer expresses 'was allowed to', either. These days *might* appears in very similar contexts as *may*, with the exception that, for some speakers, it is more tentative. There is less certainty in the sentence *I think he might come* than *I think he may come*. You could think of *might* as the tentative or unreal form of *may*. And even where you find vestiges of *might* in contexts of permission, there is this same tentativeness. A polite request like *Might I ask for another piece of cake*? is very indirect. In fact, these days I suspect most people might look at you a little strangely if you formed your request this way: it's just a little too over the top! I also suspect that in many varieties of English (certainly in my own Australian English) the distinction in tentativeness between *may* and *might* is also on the way out. I no longer see a great difference between *he may be wrong* or *he might be wrong*.

Verbs like *may* and *might*, together with *can, could, will, would, shall, should* and *must* have now established themselves as a separate group of verbs known as modals. They all deal with notions like possibility, probability, doubt and desire. They're extremely complex and there is a lot of dialectal variation. Be grateful I've spared you details of double modal constructions such as *I might could do it*, not to mention triple modals such as *I will might could do it*!

May versus can

It's difficult to talk about *may* without also considering its close mate *can*. It seems that over the years both verbs have been playing a game of linguistic tag. Originally, *can* had the meaning of 'to have the intellectual power, to know (how to do something)', so it involved mental ability rather than physical ability. An example from Old English would be *He cann ridan* ('he knows how to ride'). A later example is the famous Lovelace quotation 'Yet can I Musick too' (*Poems* 1659). The 'knowing' sense is also preserved in fixed expressions such as *to can by heart* 'to know (something) by heart' or *to can one's good* 'to know what is good for one' – also in *canny* 'clever'. However, by 1700 this sense had declined and *can* had virtually taken over the ability sense from *may*. At this time a sentence such as *he can ride* meant 'he is able to ride'.

However, these verbs never stand still for long. Since the early 19th century *can* has also acquired a permission sense, encroaching once again on the semantic turf of *may*. These days a question such as *Can I leave?* is ambiguous between ability and permission, although the permission sense is probably stronger. Some speakers feel a little squeamish about this. But the fact is, *may* has now become an extremely formal and polite expression of permission and *You may leave* now sounds a tad pompous, at least in my variety of English. The question *May I leave?* can show deference, but in Australian English probably sounds more tongue-in-cheek.

I daresay!

Many of the relics that exist in Modern English involve frozen expressions of some kind. One I had cause to think about recently is the phrase *I daresay*, meaning something like 'I'm venturing to assert or presume'. In early English it looked as if the two verbs *dare* and *say* were fusing to become a single word, the verb *to daresay* with the unified meaning 'to assume'. Take its past tense forms, for instance. Although people continued to say things such as *He durst say* or *He dared say*, in some dialects you could also find the past forms *daresayed* or *daresaid*. These last two examples demonstrate that people were thinking of the verbs as a single word.

But today it's become a very curious expression indeed. Why, for example, can't we say any more *He dares say* or even *He daresays*? We can't put the expression into the past either, or any other time frame for that matter. *I dared say* sounds awful, I *daresaid* even worse. It's only the speaker, it seems, who can *daresay* and he or she can't *daresay* at any other time than right now. *I daresay* appears to have become some sort of frozen expression, dare I say?

In fact, it's now joined that group of fixed expressions called discourse particles. These are features of talk that include phrases like *you know, I mean, I think* and a whole heap of others. I know people often sneer at these expressions, imagining them to be the sorts of things we plonk down when we've nothing better to say. But these discourse particles play crucial roles in conversational interaction and politeness. For instance, our conversations are dotted with little phrases indicating that what we are saying may not be the whole truth. Perhaps we're going on rumour or conjecture, or expressing an opinion without sufficient evidence or proof. *I daresay* has joined phrases like *I guess* and *I think* that float freely about in a sentence to express a speaker's degree of commitment to what is being discussed. They might imply imprecision or uncertainty, or they might simply be used to soften impact. For example, a few nights ago when I was being given a lift home I heard myself saying, 'I think it's left here'. Now, I knew where I lived, there was no approximation or imprecision involved. The phrase *I think* is one of those typical hedging expressions used in

117

informal contexts to reduce the force of an utterance – often simply to minimize the distance between people and create friendliness. When you consider these sorts of phrases, never think of them literally. By saying *I think* in this way, speakers aren't asserting their beliefs. This is not the literal sense of *think*. Similarly, with *I daresay*. It's nothing to do with the literal sense of *daring*. It means you think something is likely and therefore you're venturing to say something about it. *I daresay* is now of course fairly formal. These days we're perhaps more likely to write it than say it, and it's probably an endangered discourse marker.

Finally, next time you go past a sign that reads *Beware of the dog!* or *Beware the dog!* you might also reflect on this other linguistic relic. Like *I daresay*, this is more debris that doesn't behave at all well in the modern language. Try doing something else with it. *He bewares the dog*, for example, or even *he is ware of the dog*. *Beware* looks like a verb, but like *daresay* it's become a very constricted one.

'Do I dare to eat a peach'?

 This verb *dare*, even without *say*, is an odd little word. To begin with, it leads a kind of linguistic double life. On one hand, it's a fairly ordinary verb meaning 'to challenge' and it does all the sorts of things ordinary verbs do. An example would be *He dared me*. On the other hand, *dare* also behaves like modal verbs such as *may, might, can* and *could*. Here it always has another verb in tow and works more like an auxilary, or helping, verb. For example, *He dared me (to) do it*. Modals are complex verbs that express an array of concepts to do with unreality – notions of doubt, possibility, probability and contingency. They are peculiar in their grammar too. *Dare* is actually not yet a full member of this class. Sometimes it's called a 'marginal modal', but I prefer the description 'quasi modal'. Either label, *dare* hovers between being an ordinary garden-variety verb meaning 'to challenge' and one of these more abstract and grammatically complex verbs conveying a judgement about likelihood – and it's this double life that gives rise to some fairly eccentric behaviour. Consider how it forms a negative. Do you say *I daren't* (pronounced 'darent' or 'dairnt'), *I dare not,* or *I don't dare*? How do you form a question with *dare*? TS Eliot might have chosen to phrase the question in *The Love Song of J. Alfred Prufrock* as 'Do I dare to eat a peach?', but some of you might prefer 'Dare I eat a peach?' The word order is different, and it's also variable whether or not you follow *dare* with *to*.

Colloquial English is full of these quasi modals. The verb *need* is one, and so are contracted expressions such as *gonna, wanna* and *hafta.* But one of my current favourites is *better* as in *I better do it.* Though commonly heard, this little modal is rare in writing. But you occasionally find it. Here's one example I came across in a magazine: 'I better pull over here at Bourke Street rank'. The tag question shows us that *better* is behaving like a verb here: 'I better pull over, bettern't I?' OK, it's still non-standard usage. But recall one of the definitions of *weed* given earlier: 'A weed is a plant whose virtues are yet to be discovered'. It also took a few years for speakers to appreciate the virtues of 'horrid neoligisms' like *to contact* and *to notice*!

Weeds in Our Sounds and Spelling

A really long day of weeding is a restful experience, and quite changes the current of thought. For some people it is more efficient than a rest cure... After such a day my fingers are bleeding, knees tottering, back bent, dress muddy and soaking, and shoes an offence to my tidy maid; but I have attained the most profound inward peace, and the blessed belief of having uprooted all my enemies.

Anna Lea Merritt *An Artist's Garden* 1908

Evidence for early pronunciations

Before I start looking at some of our phonological weeds, let me address something that I know puzzles many people about pronunciations of the past. How do we figure out the early pronunciation of words in our language? We have no time machine to take us back through history to investigate the spoken language of our forbears. And we can't drag Old and Middle English speakers out of cold storage and ask them.

Yet we can be quite confident about early English pronunciations. The evidence comes from a number of different sources. For a start, we know a good deal about the workings of articulation and therefore also about how sounds change. We have a good idea of what are likely and unlikely sound changes, for instance. We also have dialect material at our disposal. Dialects can be conservative, and often shed light on pronunciations that have disappeared elsewhere.

Spelling also offers nice clues. Basically, the older the document, the more reliable – before spelling became standardized it could tell us a lot about the writer's pronunciation. However, even later, when spelling was starting to be fixed in printed books, it still took a long while to settle down to the conventional spellings we know today. So when Shakespeare spelt *rustle* 'russle' we can be pretty sure that the 't' had already stopped being pronounced at that time. And, of course, not everyone (fortunately for us) could spell. The private letters and documents of even very educated people contain a good many instructive 'misspellings'. Otto Jespersen, in his historical account of English sounds, gives some lovely examples. Because Queen Elizabeth I spelt *sweet* 'swit' and *deep* 'dipe', we know that the vowel change to the 'ee' sound we now pronounce in the modern language must have already taken place, at least for some speakers. We know, too, from spellings of *walk* as 'wauk', that the 'l' sound was disappearing from certain words as early as 1500.

Even more revealing are so-called 'inverse spellings' or 'backspellings'. These are a kind of spelling over-correction, where people transfer letters to words where they are not historically warranted. For example, because in 1400 people started to spell the word *write* as 'wright', we know that the guttural consonant originally represented by 'gh' must have been disappearing, at least for certain speakers. Writers were clearly losing the feel for where 'gh' did and didn't belong. (At this time they were also omitting the 'gh' from words such as *night* that did have this sound; spellings like 'nite' are also clues to when it disappeared!) Another example is the word *delight*. Again, the 'gh' spelling is not etymologically justified – it was an afterthought, but in this case it stuck. It's interesting that the *delite* of advertising-speak today is actually an earlier spelling and historically more correct!

Another example of an inverse spelling is the re-spelling of *solemn* by Shakespeare as 'solembe'. This tells us two things. One, speakers must have stopped pronouncing the 'n' from the end of *solemn* and other words such as *damn* and *condemn*. Two, it tells us that 'b's must also have been dropping off the ends of words around this time. As soon as people started putting unhistorical 'b's at the ends of words such as *solemn*, *thumb* and *crumb*, then we know that the real 'b' sounds at the end of *climb* and *comb* must have been on the way out.

We can also learn a lot from poetry and rhyming. Early poets, you'll find, are a much more reliable guide than more modern ones. They didn't go in for the eye-rhyming you find today where words correspond in spelling but not in pronunciation, such as *love* and *move*. If early poets rhymed words, then we can be pretty sure of their pronunciation likeness. For instance, Shakespeare, like many in the 16th and 17th centuries, rhymed words like *arm, harm* and *warm*. These words would have all been pronounced with an 'ah' vowel sound during this time. The change that shifted *warm* to the pronunciation we know today must have occurred some time later. The word *horse* once used to be pronounced 'hross' (to rhyme with the personal name Ross, its linguistic relative). Evidence for this pronunciation exists in nursery rhymes such as 'ride a cockhorse to Banbury Cross'. It's a lousy rhyme these days, of course!

Even better evidence comes from the manuals of phoneticians, grammarians and spelling reformers that began to appear in 16th century. When these writers started to strongly advocate pronunciations, you can be pretty sure that these weren't the pronunciations out there on the street. Let me pass on what someone writing in the 1700s had to say about dropping vowels: 'Those who wish to pronounce elegantly must be particularly attentive to the unaccented vowels; as a neat pronunciation of these forms is one of the greatest beauties of speaking'. I think it's safe to say that if the authorities were insisting on keeping these vowels, we can assume that ordinary people probably weren't. Descriptions like these of what was and wasn't 'elegant', backed up by metrical evidence from verse and drama, make it clear that words like *desperate* and *several* were losing their vowels at this time and the reduced pronunciations 'des'prate' and 'sev'ral' were on the way in.

Or take once more the business of the disappearing 'l' in words such as *walk* and *talk*. John Wallis, in his 1653 *Grammar of the English Language*, condemned what have become our current-day pronunciations of these words as slovenly (or 'negligentius', as he put it). He recommended the 'l-ful' pronunciations, or pronunciations of *walk* and *talk* to rhyme with the first syllable of the word *Balkan*. At the beginning of his book he writes (in Latin, mind you) that he is describing the 'pure and genuine pronunciation of the English language' and not (as he also put it) 'individual local dialects, or the absurdities affected by flighty women or other such barbarisms'. Lists of early barbarisms are in fact very revealing. They usually make for excellent Modern English. As is so often the case, yesterday's vulgarisms are today's standard. More weeds out of place!

Triggers for sound change – climate, ethnic character or bad dentistry?

Over time, sounds will vanish, brand-new ones will appear and old ones change their shape. Why does this happen? The theories proposed over the years to account for consonant and vowel changes have been many and varied – some wildly imaginative, many quite wacky. Let me begin with some of the more bizarre accounts of the past. They're not completely dead and buried, unfortunately, and do occasionally make a reappearance in popular accounts of language change.

Early theories sometimes linked sound change with changes in the anatomical structure of the organs of articulation. Indeed, at one time there was a popular theory that attributed the Australian accent to bad dentistry – ill-fitting dentures, in fact. Some writers even talked about a national nose inflammation through excessive amounts of pollen or hay. There is no shred of evidence for these kinds of theories. OK, there have been some extraordinary instances where mutilation of the articulatory organs probably has resulted in sound change – it's difficult to pronounce sounds made with two lips if you have a large disk inserted in one of them. But cases of this nature are extremely rare.

Ethnic character was another theory that was bandied about. Again, to take the Australian accent as an example, I recall one early account that attributed our speech to a kind of gross national inferiority complex. Or how about a free-wheeling and adventurous spirit – an outlaw heritage perhaps? These have all been put forward at some time to account for the Aussie accent.

People have also argued that geographical and climactic conditions influence sound systems. Very popular was the notion that somehow harsh climates produced harsh sounds – not that harsh sounds were ever clearly defined, although 'guttural' sounds were often implied. So what do we do with the Aboriginal languages of central Australia, I wonder? Here the climate is about as harsh as you can get, and yet the sound inventories of these languages contain none of these so-called harsh guttural sounds. So if language change is not caused by climate, ethnic character, anatomy, or bad dentistry for that matter, what does motivate sound inventories to shift?

Let me address one popular theory for which there is support and that is the notion of simplicity. In all the languages of the world you will find sounds dropping out of words, or merging over time, or often altering their shape to be more like neighbouring sounds. These sorts of changes do involve a lessening in muscular effort. I've mentioned this before with respect to very common words. When you find yourself saying the same word again and again, the gestures of articulation become automatic, and when things become automatic we reduce them. It's been described as economy of effort, following the line of least resistance, human laziness, carelessness, sloth – but the result is also a more efficient, more stream-lined production. However you choose to view it, simplicity is a factor.

Nonetheless, simplicity can't account for all types of sound change. There are plenty of changes that actually result in greater complexity. Take the two English sounds in the middle of the words *either* and *ether*. In writing, we've only got one symbol for them, unfortunately, and that's 'th'. These are both rare sounds in the world's languages – foreign students of English have terrible trouble with them, children take a long time to acquire them and plenty of English varieties such as Cockney and Irish have done away with them. And yet English has acquired these two particularly tricky sounds out of something much more straightforward. So, why?

And there's another problem for the simplicity argument. It can't account for the fact that many changes don't take place. For instance, it's easier to pronounce a 'g' as 'y' between vowels. Spanish has made this change. Pennsylvania German has too. So why hasn't English? Later I will discuss how it is natural for 's' to change to 'r' when it is flanked by vowels. So why don't we do this all the time? Why do these sorts of simplicity changes happen only in some languages, not all, and why do they occur only some of the time?

Finally, there's a difficulty with the whole notion of simplicity. Changes can bring about a more straightforward sound system, but complicate things considerably elsewhere, especially in grammar. Frequently, sound changes hurtle gleefully through the language making life simpler with respect to pronunciation, but with no regard for the grammatical system, which is often left in tatters. Many of the irregularities in Modern English grammar (such as *was–were*, *foot–feet* and *wife–wives*) are debris washed up after a sound change has taken place.

So yes, simplicity is a factor, but it's not the only one. In sound change, indeed in any language change, the driving forces are numerous and complex. They involve a network of different social, psychological and linguistic pressures – and of course external or foreign influences, too. There are linguists, I admit, who argue that linguistic change is totally frivolous, without system, entirely random and completely unpredictable. Yet it's a fact that languages remain highly structured systems. If language change were totally capricious, as these people argue, this would not be the case.

Sugar! Shoot! Shucks!

Sometimes sound changes are completely deliberate. It can happen, for example, that speakers intentionally distort the pronunciation of words to disguise something that is offensive. It's a way of saying a word without really having to say it. Perhaps you want to use a swear word to let off steam, but you happen to be in polite company. Society provides you with an out in the form of euphemistic remodellings like *Shivers! Shoot! Shucks!* or *Shite!* The original English word for 'rabbit' was *coney*. It rhymed with *money* and *honey* but its phonological proximity to the female unmentionable body part was for many speakers just too close for comfort. Before it dropped out of use in the late 19th century, it was remodelled in some places to distance itself from the taboo homonym. This distorted pronunciation is preserved in the placename *Coney Island*. It's also likely that the word *bunny* is another coy remodelling of *coney*. *Playboy*'s 'bunnies' and 'Bunny Club' follow a long tradition from 18th-century London's 'Cunny House'. Similarly affected are some words containing *cock*, especially names; for example, many people with the surname *Koch* give their surname a spelling pronunciation 'kotch' just to make sure it's linguistically far enough away from another offending body part. (One such person was Ed Koch, a former mayor of New York.) In the same way, *Alcox* gets remodelled to *Alcott*.

Another taboo act is 'to take the Lord's name in vain'. In response to this taboo we produce remodelled expressions like *gosh, golly, cor, gorblimey, gordonbennet, gordon-'ighlanders, goodness, goodness knows, (good) gracious, for goodness sake, zounds, by gad, gog, cod* and so on. Many of these are very old. They first appeared during the Renaissance in response to injunctions introduced against blasphemy and profanity on the stage. As usual, censorship and repression simply had the effect of fostering people's ingenuity. You'll find this period coincides with a flourishing of new profane and blasphemous language in the form of hundreds of camouflaged oaths. Expressions disguising Jesus Christ are also plentiful: *Jeeze, gee, gee whizz, by jingo, jeepers creepers, jiminy cricket, christmas, cripes, crust, crumbs, crikey, by jove* and also *for crying out loud* (an ingenious remodelling of the expression 'for Christ sake').

It was queasiness about this kind of linguistic masquerade that triggered the fall from grace of the word *bloody*. Early on in its life, *bloody* was not a bad word at all, but a folk etymology arose that derived it from a remodelling of the expression *By our lady*, an oath calling on the assistance of the Virgin Mary. At first blush this sounds plausible, especially when you consider the spectacular remodellings that produced *strewth* from 'God's truth', *heck* from 'hell' and *drat* from 'God rot'. But *By our lady* is most certainly not the source of *bloody*. However, linguistic truth isn't an issue here – speakers' perceptions are what matters. So *bloody* became unmentionable, often rendered invisible as *b****y*. Its unmentionableness triggered a number of euphemistic remodellings such as the expletives *blimey!, blast!, blow!* and epithets *blessed, bleeding, blinking, blooming, blinding, blasted*. Many of these, you'll notice, have blasphemous and profane associations that would have come from the earlier folk etymology.

Now, all this might seem like an interesting bit of linguistic trivia. But in fact, in some parts of the world, this kind of remodelling of words is very widespread and can have far-reaching

Taboo and magical body parts

 Linguist Hans Heinrich Hock gives an interesting illustration of this kind of distortion. It involves the word for 'tongue'. Now, all humans have tongues. So there must have been a word for this body part in the parent language of the Indo-European languages. Yet we don't really know what this word would have sounded like. Particularly problematic is the nature of its first consonant. This is in itself interesting, given that usually the beginnings of words are the most stable and therefore helpful when it comes to figuring out the shape of earlier vocabulary. So why isn't it possible to recreate the word for 'tongue'? What would appear to be related words in the modern Indo-European languages have all undergone irregular and quite peculiar sound changes – sounds have swapped places mysteriously or been contaminated by semantically related words such as the verb 'to lick'. Hock offers a plausible explanation for this. Taboo. The tongue was the organ of speech, and therefore imbued with magical powers, like speech itself. As he put it, 'speech made it possible to name things or people and by naming them to have power over them'. (Think of the problems Rumplestiltskin had when the heroine discovered his name.) As odd as this sounds to us today, for our ancestors the tongue was a magical body part and subject to the same kinds of taboos as we now place on bawdy parts, bodily effluvia, sexual activities, death and disease.

consequences for the languages spoken there. For example, in traditional Austronesian societies, the death of a person renders their name taboo. These death taboos can have major effects on the ordinary vocabulary of languages when personal names are common words or derive from common words. Linguist Gary Simons describes how in a sample of fifty Austronesian languages known to have some sort of naming taboo, twenty-five have a name taboo that extends into a common word taboo. In a further eighteen languages, words even resembling the tabooed names are themselves taboo. In some parts of the Solomon Islands as much as 59 per cent of the basic vocabulary is potentially taboo for some people on the island. The consequence of these death taboos is a massive turnover of vocabulary items. There are also weird irregular sound changes. Sounds turn up in odd places. They mutate unexpectedly. Words are often funny-looking. These speakers are remodelling words in much the same way that we transform *fuck* to *fudge* and *hell* to *heck*. But the changes are much more widespread and not as sporadic as in the English examples. They make it very difficult to determine the chronology of linguistic changes that have occurred. Even the genetic relationships between languages can be obscured – the vocabulary, even core vocabulary, is just too unstable.

Foreign accents

When you grow up speaking English in a place like Australia, it's easy to think that monolingualism is somehow normal and that those who are bilingual or multilingual are part of a very special group of people. But this is not the case. When you look at speech communities all round the world, you quickly realize that bilingualism is the more usual state of affairs.

Many of you will be bilingual, perhaps even multilingual, in other words, you'll have command of more than one or even two languages. But defining bilingualism is not as straightforward as you might think. Proficiency can range from a native-like ability in two languages to what could be described as a more passive knowledge of a second language – perhaps it can be understood, but not spoken. In fact, true native-like fluency in more than one language is rare. Typically you'll find that one language is dominant and it often interferes with the other language. Take the matter of a foreign accent, probably the most obvious kind of interference occurring between languages. Foreign accents arise because speakers transfer the articulatory habits of one language to another. But there are different ways this can happen.

Very evident is when one sound gets substituted for another. Speakers of Slavic languages, for example, will find a very different 'r' sound when they come to speak Australian English. Our 'r' is more sonorant or vowel-like, while the 'r' sound in Slavic languages is a trill made with the tip of the tongue. Speakers will typically seek out the best match possible, and it's often fascinating to see which sounds they perceive as being the closest ones available in their language to substitute when speaking the second language.

For example, English has those rather difficult sounds that we represent as 'th' in words such as *thin* and *then*. These sounds are known as dental fricatives, so-called because when the tongue makes contact with the upper incisors the movement of air can be heard – there's friction. Both these sounds are rare in the other languages and they cause problems for non-native speakers. A French speaker typically substitutes 's' and 'z', so *thin* and *them* come out as 'sin' and 'zem'. A Russian speaker, though, will substitute 't' and 'd', so *thin* and *them* become 'tin' and 'dem'. It's interesting that these two groups of speakers make different choices here. The French with their 'sin' and 'zem' have opted to keep the fricative nature of the English sounds; the air turbulence we hear in our two 'th' sounds is maintained in 's' and 'z'. Russian speakers could have done likewise, but for some reason they must consider this feature unimportant. So instead they opt for 't' and 'd'. It's a bit of a puzzle sometimes what sounds end up being substituted, and we have to look closely at the sound systems of languages to figure out why speakers choose the sounds they do.

What also contributes to a foreign accent is when certain pronunciation rules in the dominant or primary language are transferred into the second language. German, for example, has evolved a rule whereby certain sounds at the ends of words become voiceless. English doesn't happen to have this particular rule, but German speakers will often transfer it when they speak English. The word *have* for instance gets pronounced 'haf', *old* as 'olt'. Or take a Spanish-English bilingual speaker when it comes to pronouncing nasal sounds. In English we have three nasal sounds – 'm', 'n' and the nasal sound we represent as 'ng'. All three nasals can occur at the ends of words, as in 'some', 'son' and 'sung'. This is not the case in Spanish, however. Only one nasal sound, namely 'n', can occur in this position. So it's tricky for a Spanish speaker learning English to identify and also pronounce the other nasal sounds when they are word-final, because their language has this restriction. In Spanish you'd never encounter words such as 'some' and 'sung'.

Other aspects of a sound system can be imposed on a second language and contribute to a foreign accent. Languages have rules that describe the permissible sequences of vowels and consonants in a syllable. These are called phonotactic constraints. Finnish, for example, tolerates only a single consonant at the beginning of a word, but in English it's possible to find even three-consonant clusters in word-initial position – such as 'spl' as in *splash*, 'str' in *stretch* and 'scr' as in *scrunch*.

But probably what contributes most strongly to a perceived foreign accent is the transference of stress and intonation patterns. These are the features that children acquire first: they are the most 'deeply anchored', if you like. So it's not surprising that these are the most readily transferred from a first to a second language. Even highly accomplished bilinguals with native-like fluency in both languages often give themselves away by distinctive intonation and stress patterns. Indeed, it's often precisely these features that survive as evidence that what is now a monolingual community has developed from an earlier bilingual one. Think of the distinctive forms of English now spoken in the former Celtic-speaking areas of Britain. Whereas interference patterns usually only remain as long as the group itself remains bilingual, intonation and stress patterns linger longer.

Hyperforeignisms

The ABC's Standing Committee on Spoken English puts out a monthly report wherein members discuss certain thorny issues to do with English usage. One SCOSE report raises the tricky business of pronouncing foreign proper names, especially those involving consonants and vowels that don't appear in the inventory of English sounds. One example given recently was the current tendency to mispronounce the Chinese city *Beijing* with the rather French sounding consonant 'zh'; in other words, 'Beizhing'.

This seems to me to be a fine example of a phenomenon known as hyperforeignism. As linguists Hock and Joseph have described it, certain sounds take on exotic associations for English speakers, and they often overuse these sounds in words they know to be foreign – hence the description hyperforeignism. One such sound is the 'zh' sound which we've acquired from French words such as *rouge, beige* and *genre*. It appeared in the English sound system only fairly recently, principally via these borrowings, and it is still a very restricted consonant. Because it has a rather exotic ring to it, we tend to plop it into other words we know are also borrowings. Foreign words, after all, have to sound foreign! Take the Indian words *raj* meaning 'rule or dominion' as in *the British raj*, and *rajah* meaning 'king or prince'. Both often get mispronounced as 'razh' and 'razha'. The pronunciations 'radj' and 'radja' have the boring old English sound 'dj' (as in *judge*). They just don't sound as exotic. Others that receive this same pronunciation are foreign words like *cashmere* – 'cazhmere' – and occasionally also *kosher* – 'kozher'. I suggest this is also what's going on here with the pronunciation of *Beijing* as 'Beizhing'. The 'dj' consonant would be closer to the Chinese original, but it has a rather mundane English ring to it. This foreign city should have a foreign sound to it; so 'zh' is substituted.

Further examples of hyperforeignisms in English are expressions like *no problemo*. The actual Spanish word for 'problem' ends in 'a' not 'o', but for English speakers 'o' is the quintessential Spanish ending – after all, we have loan words like *taco, nacho* and *burrito*. (There's also the pleasing rhyming aspect to *no problemo*.) French borrowings are particularly prone to this sort of overuse. If speakers know anything at all about French, they know that a consonant at the end of a word is silent. Take the French word *trait* that we've borrowed to describe a 'distinguishing feature or quality'. It sounds far more posh to pronounce it as 'tray' rather than 'trait' – in other words, closer to the original French. The trouble is, speakers over-extend this pronunciation rule and remove final consonants from the ends of all words they know to be French – even those ones the French themselves pronounce. The actual facts of the foreign language aren't important: it's what sounds good that matters! The SCOSE report has a lovely example of this. Apparently a broadcaster was heard to pronounce *Russian roulette* as 'Russian rooh-lay' – as the SCOSE report concludes, a little French can be a dangerous thing!

Mrs Gafoops – a hyperforeignism?

 Mrs Gafoops came up in conversation recently. Someone was trying to recall a woman's name and referred instead to Mrs Gafoops (or Kafoops). So who was she? She certainly appears in a number of non-mainstream collections like Partridge's *Dictionary of Slang*, but none of the lexicographers seems game to offer any explanation. Partridge himself simply states that it's been Australian English since the 1930s and is used for 'any woman not named'. But why Gafoops?

My first thought was that it probably came about along the pattern of the other *ker-* or *ge-* words you often find in comic books – *kerbang, kerbiff, kerbonk, kaboom, kerflop, kerplop*, to give just a few. But these are all somehow imitative of the impact or sound of something, which makes them different from the *gafoops* in Mrs Gafoops. My second thought was that Gafoops was invented on the pattern of a kind of quasi or mock German. For many English speakers the prefix *ge-* is what makes the German language German. So someone wanting to mock German speakers might say something like 'the cow has over the fence gejumped'. Of course, the verb at the end of the sentence is another earmark of German. Apparently there used to be a number of German comedians in the United States who manufactured this kind of mock German and this gave rise to sham German words like *geflop* and *gesplash*. So could this be the source for the *gafoops* in Mrs Gafoops? Well, it seems plausible to me!

Gnawing and gnashing; knowing and knitting

Over the years English has been simplifying the clusters of consonants it allows, in particular the clusters that occur at the beginning of syllables. Take, for instance, the combination 'wr', retained in the spelling of words such as *wrong* and *written*. Sometime during the 16th century the 'w' stopped being pronounced. It took a while to complete (sound changes are never fast), but by 1700 the 'wr' cluster was pretty well dead and buried. This change left us with a number of homophones: different words pronounced in the same way, such as *write* as in 'express in writing' and *right* as in 'correct'.

A couple of consonant clusters managed to hang in there a little longer, namely 'kn' and 'gn', preserved again in the spelling of words like *know* and *knit*, *gnaw* and *gnash*. The loss of these clusters, we know, must have begun sometime during the 17th century. But as Roger Lass describes in his historical account of early Modern English sounds, 'k' and 'g' didn't suddenly disappear. In a sense, they faded away. For instance, several sources around that time give the pronunciation of 'kn' in certain words as 'tn'. Here, rather than disappearing altogether, 'k' changes to 't' to be more like the following 'n' (both 't' and 'n' are pronounced in the same place in the mouth). It's a weakening process that signals that the sound was on the way out. There were other signs that 'k' was losing its integrity: for example, the pronunciation of the name *Twickenham* as 'Twitnam'. But back to the 'kn' in *knee*, *know* and *knit*. The eventual disappearance of 'k' in words such as these left us with another pile of homophones – words with the same pronunciation – such as *knead* 'to work dough' versus *need* 'to require', or the medieval *knight* versus the *night* between sunrise and sunset.

Compared to the reduction of the 'kn' cluster, the disappearance of 'g' before 'n' seems to have been a little faster. One pronouncing dictionary from as early as 1640 is quite explicit. In words such as *gnat*, *gnaw* and *gnu*, the writer declares, 'G in this combination inclines to the force of N'. Presumably he means, it's gone! Occasionally the cluster was protected by a preceding vowel. For example, *agnostic* preserves the 'gn' lost in related *gnostic* (just as *acknowledgment* preserves the 'kn' that has been lost from related *know* and *knowledge*).

This simplification of clusters is still going on. Two that are high on the endangered list are clusters involving 'h'. One is definitely a lost cause. This is the cluster you find, or rather you once found, in words like *which*, *white* and *what*. The early pronunciation was something like 'hw' (indeed, the cluster was originally spelt this way, but changed to 'wh' sometime after the Norman

Conquest). We know that the change in pronunciation from 'hw' to 'w' started in the south of England as early as the Middle Ages, but it couldn't have been a big hit, since the 'hw' cluster went across to North America in the 17th century. In the 18th century, though, the pronunciation 'w' was clearly gaining ground. It had even begun to creep into the speech of the educated, who had earlier condemned it. (Walker, for example, in his *Critical Pronouncing Dictionary* of 1791 declares the pronunciation of *what* as 'wot' a 'feeble Cockney pronunciation'.) By 1800 *which* and *witch* and *whether* and *weather* had become homophones in Standard English pronunciation. The cluster is managing to hang in there in places like Scotland and Ireland, but everywhere else it's well and truly on the way out.

Wlat, hring, hneck and hloud

When printing arrived in the late 1400s, English spelling started to settle down – until then there were no guidelines, so people spelt as they liked. My collection of recipes from the 14th century, for example, spells *ginger* in nine different ways – everything from *ginge* to *gyngyuyr*! There was no correct way to spell ginger at that time. Then, just as spelling started to regularize, the language experienced a number of significant sound changes. Many sounds altered their shape, and many disappeared altogether. As a result we now have thousands of words spelt much as they were pronounced in Geoffrey Chaucer's time. Most vexing are, of course, those silent letters in words such as *write*, *right*, *sword*, *know*, *gnat* – the bane of all unfortunate students of the English language today.

If pronunciation changes happened early enough, though, the spelling had a better chance of reflecting them. For example, 'w' before 'l' disappeared sometime during the late medieval period. Unlike a later change that saw 'w' disappear before 'r' (as in *write*), this change was early enough to appear in the spelling of words. People once used to write *lisp* with a 'w' at the beginning.

In fact, if you check in *The Oxford English Dictionary* you'll still find a handful of words beginning with 'wl', but all of them, sadly, obsolete. They include the noun *wlat*, meaning 'loathing or disgust', and *wlonk*, meaning 'proud or haughty'. Around the same time we were losing this 'wl' cluster, we were losing 'h' from a number of clusters as well. For example, Modern English *loud* comes from Old English *hlud* (the 'hl' at that time would have been pronounced a bit like the Welsh 'l' in Llewellyn); *ring* comes from *hring*; and *neck* from *hnecca* (this 'hn' would have sounded something like a sniff).

If the printer Caxton had been born a couple of centuries later, or if these sound changes had occurred a couple of centuries earlier, our spelling would be much truer to pronunciation.

The other 'h' cluster on the endangered list is the 'hy' you hear at the beginning of words such as *huge* and *human*. Many speakers have already lost this one as well. For these people, the name *Hugh* and pronoun *you* are both pronounced as 'yew', *human* and *Yuman* (a North American Indian language) as 'yewman'. With the 'hl', 'hr' and 'hn' clusters now gone and 'hw' on its last legs, 'hy' is the last of the exotic (h)aitch combinations – but its days are clearly numbered.

Disappearing syllables – the case of February

'We keep hearing all these callow voices on TV and radio mouthing about FebYuary', complains one Queensland resident bitterly. 'Don't they know', he continues, 'that this is the only month with two Rs?' What this person is complaining about here is a process known as haplology. It's a change that involves the loss of sounds, a common enough process in speech. However, in the special case of haplology, the change involves an entire syllable. Typically it happens when that syllable occurs near another syllable that is either identical or at least very similar. For instance, haplology is itself a word that has in the middle two 'lo' syllables side by side. So if I were to pronounce haplology as 'haplogy' this would illustrate exactly the process involved.

The history of English has a number of well-known examples of haplology, to many of which we no longer give a thought. The most famous occurs in the name England itself. This was originally *Anglaland*, meaning the Land of the Angles (the Angles being one of the Germanic tribes that settled in Britain over a thousand years ago, and who brought with them the ancestor of Modern English). *Anglaland* has two 'la' syllables side by side, but haplology has reduced them to one and given us the name *England*. The same process produced *Poland* from *Poleland* sometime during the 16th century. In Old and Middle English the word *eighteen* used to have four syllables and the word *eighty* had three. Both words have undergone a number of different changes, one of which involves the loss of the middle 'ta' syllable. *Eighteen* would have been pronounced something like 'achteteene' and *eighty* as 'achteti' (with the 'ch' representing the same gutteral sound that appears at the end of German *ach*). Similarly, *honestetee* with four syllables was reduced to current-day *honesty* with three syllables. These days, it's much more usual to hear 'probly' than *probably*.

This process of haplology is typically quite rare and fairly sporadic in nature. However, there is one occasion in English where it occurs regularly. What's more, it's not confined to colloquial speech, but is part of the standard written language. This reduction occurs where you add an *-ly* ending to a word that already ends in an 'l' – one syllable will always be pruned. Back in the 14th century Chaucer might well have written *humblely* with three syllables, but nowadays we pronounce this (and also write it) as *humbly*, with just two syllables. Similarly, we say *nobly, simply, idly* and *gently* – all have been cropped of a syllable.

This brings me back to the dreaded second month of the year pronounced 'February'. This pronunciation takes considerable effort, and in normal rapid speech we're likely to drop the first 'r' and pronounce it 'Febyuary'. More likely still we'll reduce it by one syllable to 'Febyury', or even by two in the case of 'Febry'. These pronunciations bring *February* in line with the month of *January*. It's common for words that occur in a list to affect each other's pronunciation in this way. Numerals are particularly susceptible to this. The English word *four*, for example, should begin with 'wh', but 'wh' changed to 'f' because it was 'contaminated' by the following number *five*.

However, there's another problem with February and that's the succession of 'rs.' Sonorous sounds like 'l' and 'r' are notoriously unstable and prone to change, especially when there's a number of them appearing together. The pronunciations 'Febyury' and 'Febry' still seem to attract ferocious criticism and yet, if you look at the language, you'll find a close succession of 'r's will regularly trigger this sort of change and usually it goes undetected. Words like *library, temporary* and *literary*, for instance, will usually reduce to 'lib(e)ry', 'temp(e)ry' and 'lit(e)ry'. At least one syllable will drop, in fact in normal rapid speech, usually more. These aren't new pronunciations by any means. The 19th-century novelist William Thackeray used to spell these words with a syllable missing – 'tempory', for example, and 'littery'. These changes have attracted little attention, and it seems a tad unfair to me that poor old 'Febry' should get such bad press. Our language is full of such occurrences. No one would dream of restoring the extra syllables to *Sunday* and *Monday* by resurrecting 'Sunnenday' and 'Monenday'. It seems that changes of this nature are only ever odious when they're happening under your nose.

Illusion versus allusion

'Why can't people distinguish between *illusion* and *allusion*?' complains talkback caller Bob of Bermagui. One of the difficulties here is that the vowel sounds at the start of these words are unstressed, and in ordinary conversation it's normal for us to reduce them to something that sounds much like 'ugh'. If we didn't, we'd sound quite artificial and rather precious. And we've been doing it for as long as English has been recorded – at least a thousand years.

We know this because of the confused spelling of these early times. Sometimes the reduced vowel was written with 'i', sometimes with 'u', sometimes with 'e'. People just weren't sure, because in pronunciation the distinction between these vowel sounds was neutralized when they were unstressed. And, of course, there were no dictionaries around to help out.

Weak vowels not only weaken, they frequently delete. Think of the pronunciations of words such as *interest, every* and *family*. Few people these days would insist on 'int**e**rest', 'ev**e**ry' and 'fam**i**ly'. But there is a lot of variation, especially between British English and American English. As is so often the case, the newer form without the vowel is British and the older form American. Hence 'med'cine' is British, 'med**i**cine', American. Australian English, as usual, hovers in between and can go both ways. Although 'med**i**cine' is probably more common, Australians normally side with British English and delete the vowel. Think of pronunciations like 'gen'ral', 'sev'ral', 'monast'ry' and 'batt'ry'. It's rare that you hear the vowels in the middle of these words.

We've been losing unstressed vowels for centuries. If the loss occurs far enough back it will be reflected in the spelling. We no longer spell *lobster* as *lobbester*, as it was once, and *chapter* is no longer *chapiter*. In proper names you often find both spellings – think of *Kathryn* and *Catherine*. When both forms hang around, the forms occasionally split and go their separate ways – sometimes dramatically. For example, *fantasy* and *fancy* are historically the same word. *Fancy* was originally simply a contracted form of *fantasy*. In the same way, *curtsy* was a shortened form of *courtesy* and *lightning* a shortened form of *lightening*. As you can see, the meanings can become sharply differentiated.

We also have striking examples involving the loss of initial vowels – *ticket* versus *etiquette*, *cute* versus *acute*, *squire* versus *esquire*, *fender* versus *defender*, *fence* versus *defense*. The first members of each of these pairs were originally merely reduced forms of the same word. The initial vowel disappeared because it was unstressed and therefore weak – it's much like when we say ''scuse me' in place of 'excuse me'.

This sort of shortening is very different from the process that turns *bicycle* into *bike* and *professor* into *prof*. This second kind is more deliberate – it also reduces whole syllables, even ones that are stressed, as in *prof* from *professor*. The type of reduction I've been talking about has to do with the linguistic heartbeat of our language – the tee-tum-tee-tum rhythm that is so characteristic of English.

Disappearing 'd's – the case of Wednesday

'You can't be happy with a woman who pronounces both 'd's in Wednesday' wrote Peter de Vries in 1981 in *Sauce for the Goose*. Indeed, in normal speech it's usual for the first 'd' in this particular day of the week to vanish. So why do we drop the 'd' in Wednesday? There are a couple of reasons.

We know from appearances of the word in early writing that the 'd' has been gone for some time. Spellings like *Wensday* were common in the 1800s. Indeed, descriptions in pronouncing dictionaries from as early as the mid-1700s show that it was mute even then. Throughout the history of English, 'd' has been prone to vanishing acts of this nature. Often it's because it finds itself in the middle of a difficult consonant cluster. Think of the pronunciation of placenames such as *Win(d)sor* and *Guil(d)ford*, or simply ordinary vocabulary items such as *frien(d)ship*, *han(d)s, han(d)some, han(d)ful, lan(d)scape* – all have lost their 'd's. It would need to be a very careful pronunciation for you to hear the 'd' in these words. The same is true of the consonant 't'. It has also dropped from many words where it occurs in awkward clusters, as in examples such as *bris(t)le, has(t)en, mois(t)en, of(t)en, Chris(t)mas* and, of course, placenames such as *Wes(t)minster*.

Notice that all the examples I've given are everyday common usage words. This sort of reduction is always more usual with ordinary vocabulary. A fine example would be the form *Mrs* from *mistress*. It also affects words that appear frequently in combination. For instance, in normal rapid speech the 't' is always dropped from combinations like *must be* and *next month*. Well-aged compound words, too, show the effects of repetition. Through frequent use the elements of the compound become more and more closely associated, and the boundaries between them blur. Just look at what's happened to the pronunciation of words like *landlord* and *grandmother*. Less familiar or less usual compounds won't show the same sort of reduction. Compare an infrequent word like *handstroke*, which usually retains the 'd', with common usage *handkerchief*, which always loses it. Less usual *postmaster* keeps its 't', compared to more usual *postman* which drops it. It's a fact of lexical life that repetition leads to reduction. No one would think of pronouncing the

't' in *hasten* – this is a combination of the word *haste* plus the ending
-en. The same would be true of *soften*. But what about the word
swift plus the same *-en* ending? *Swiften* was once a verb, but never
gained the same frequency as *hasten* and *soften* – and so it never lost
its 't'. And certainly if it ever came back from the dead its 't' would
be intact.

So why are frequently used words prone to reduction? Well,
for a start, an everyday word like *postman* or *soften* will often crop
up in casual settings where pronunciation shortcuts are more
usual. A lot can be taken for granted when you're chatting with
someone you know well in a familiar environment; you can afford
to drop a consonant or vowel here and there. Moreover, frequent
words like *postman* are also easier to access, so hearers don't
require the same amount of phonetic detail. And there's another
factor. As linguist Joan Bybee, someone who has studied closely
the effects of repetition on language, describes it, when we repeat
a word, the movements of our speech organs become automatic
and when this happens there's a reduction in their timing and
magnitude. As the speed of execution automatically increases, the
transition between sounds becomes more fluent – movements
might even overlap. A sailor who finds he has to say the word
captain often will never give it the full pronunciation – it'll always
be 'capm'. We see this in many repetitive activities, not just linguistic gestures. Think of the sailor's salute – you can be sure
there'll be shortcuts.

Sometimes these lost 'd's and 't's are restored. A good example
is the word *ordinary*. Once upon a time its shortened version
'ornery' was considered perfectly acceptable. It still has an entry in
most dictionaries, although the meaning has shifted to 'cantanker-
ous'. But an awareness of the spelling saw the full pronunciation
restored. 'Spelling pronunciations', as they're known, have become
more common because of the privileged position that writing now
occupies. If a sound appears in the spelling, speakers get the feeling
it should be pronounced. The word *often* has a 't', so some people
pronounce it 'often' not 'offen'. If you think about this, it doesn't
make a lot of sense. Letters don't have sounds: they symbolise
sounds. But writing takes centre stage and speech plays second fid-
dle. Ours has become very much a society where the writing tail
now wags the speaking dog. Forgive my mixture of metaphors!

Placenames

I've just returned from a holiday in Western Australia, and while I was there a number of people commented on the fact that outsiders, particularly those from the so-called 'Eastern States', often mispronounce West Australian placenames. Many complain, for instance, that they constantly hear 'Awlbany' for *Albany* (pronounced with the 'a' of *Allan*), 'Fr'mantle' for *Fremantle* (pronounced with the 'ee' of *free*), 'Darby' for *Derby* (pronounced with the 'er' of *herb*).

Placenames are always tricky, and there are probably a number of things going on here – all of which make it very difficult for a newcomer. Most people have had experience of spectacular examples in the UK. My aunt and uncle, for instance, lived in a place spelt *Bicester*, but for those in the know, pronounced 'bister'. Then, of course, there's that place pronounced by locals as 'sister' – not that you'd know from the spelling *Cirencester*. I used to live in a street in London called *Theobald's Road*. For a while I gave it spelling pronunciation, until one nice taxi driver put me right by politely pointing out that it was in fact 'Tibbalds Road'. I was extremely grateful. There are hundreds of such examples – Gloucester, Barnoldswick, Chiswick, Leicester, Salisbury, Shrewsbury, Worcestershire, Daventry are just some. All of them have spellings that in no way reflect their actual pronunciation.

Of course, these placenames become very effective social passwords. If you say 'Awlbany' for *Albany*, then this immediately identifies you as a dangerous outsider – certainly no Albanyite would say this. The pronunciation 'straya' for Australia suggests someone is probably from down-under and one of the gang, but the person who says 'awstralia' is definitely not! So there are social reasons for hanging onto unusual pronunciations of placenames – and the more absurd the pronunciation the more effective the password.

There are also phonetic factors involved here. You'll notice that they all involve extreme shortening. *Cirencester* with four syllables turns into 'sister' with only two. Sounds reduce, merge with neighbouring sounds or even drop out altogether. Frequency of use is probably the main reason here. As mentioned earlier, repetition has a profound effect on pronunciation. We will always make short cuts when we're in familiar territory. And shortenings sound more intimate, too. Deliberate abbreviations of placenames such as *Shep* for Shepparton, *Brum* for Birmingham or *Cott* for Cottesloe suggest we have a warm and friendly attitude towards that place. We might even add on one of those cuddly endings – *Broady* for Broadmeadows, for instance, or *Rotto* for Rottnest Island.

All this might give the impression that placenames are always changing. Not so. They can also be conservative. The pronunciation of Derby in Australia is the traditional pronunciation. Back in the 14th century a sound change took place that shifted the first vowel to 'ah'. Hence 'Dahby' is the newer pronunciation. The different pronunciations of Berkeley offer another example. As with Derby, it's probably the pressure of spelling that has restored the older pronunciation of Berkeley ('berkly') in America. It might also reflect the special power of names to do their own thing. *Stanley*, for instance, was originally a placename. Its literal meaning is 'stoney field'. The ordinary word *stone* reflects the sound change that took place centuries ago – but the name *Stanley* didn't follow suit. Names are magical things. They can change in weird and wonderful ways. But they also have the power to stand alone and resist normal changes that are going on elsewhere in the language.

Newcastle, Castlereagh Street and Castlemaine

Accent differences in Australia aren't particularly striking, especially when you compare them to, say, the United States or the United Kingdom. When they do occur here you'll find they're more likely to be a matter of statistical tendency, with certain pronunciations occurring with more frequency in one place than in another. Take the pronunciation of the word *castle* in placenames around Australia such as Castlemaine, Newcastle (Street) and Castlereagh

Street. These accent differences probably don't hold the same fascination for those outside of Australia, but I'll mention them here anyway, since they involve variation that has become very significant around the English-speaking world. Melbourne people are more likely to say 'castle' with the same 'flat a' sound as words such as *bat* and *trap*. In Brisbane you hear this pronunciation too, although it's not as common. Sydney and Hobart people are more likely to say 'cahstle' (with the same vowel sound as *calm* and *palm*), Adelaide and Perth speakers even more so. So where does this particular variation stem from? The answer lies in complex vowel changes that took place between the 17th and 19th centuries. Here's a brief history.

The oldest pronunciation is the 'flat a' sound you still hear in *bat* and *trap*. During the 17th century certain speakers in Britain started to lengthen this vowel, but not in all words. Sound change is like that. It's gradual. New pronunciations sneak through vocabulary, touching different groups of words at different times. But there is always a kind of system. It's never random. This particular change first affected words such as *path* and *grass*. Whenever the vowel 'a' appeared before consonants that had friction, such as the 'th' in *path* or the 's' in *grass*, it was lengthened. This same change then affected words where the vowel appeared before a nasal sound and a following 's' or 't' – for example, *dance* and *plant*. So around this time the vowel in all these words would have sounded much like the vowel in the middle of *band*. In other words, the pronunciations of *path, grass, dance* and *plant* would have been very close to what you now hear in North America. Then later, sometime during the 19th century, this 'a' developed into the 'ah' sound you hear in some places today – hence, the pronunciations 'pahth', 'grahss', 'dahns' and 'plahnt'.

All this is typical of sound change. A new pronunciation starts off slowly; it might then have a sudden spurt of energy and affect many words, but then often slows down, leaving a handful of words that one day may fall in line and change, but also may never do so. This particular sound change left many words unaffected. In words such as *bat* the vowel never shifted, the change just petered out. There are also a few curiosities. For instance, the pronunciation of *ass* as in 'donkey'. It should have changed, along with *grass* and *path*, to 'ahs'. We say 'grahs', so why not

143

'ahs'? The answer is probably obvious – the word would then have sounded like the body part. Presumably, speakers didn't change their pronunciation because they wanted to avoid vulgar associations with *arse*. You'll always find odd exceptions like this.

However, none of this accounts for the *castle–cahstle* variation you find in Australia. This has a different explanation. So far I've talked about the spread of a new pronunciation through the language, in other words, the inward spread of change. Changes also diffuse outwardly through the speech community. A change might start within a certain social group and then may, or may not, move to other groups. And of course the regional varieties may all be doing it at different rates, too. This particular vowel change happens to be one of the great divides in English dialectology. In the UK you have differences between the North and North Midlands and the South and South Midlands. While the North has the older 'flat a' pronunciation for words such as *path* and *grass*, places south, such as London, have 'pahth' and 'grahs'. The USA is the most conservative. The pronunciation you hear in General American English is the older 'flat a'. The colonization of America took place during the 17th century, before the pronunciation change that shifted 'path' to 'pahth' and 'grass' to 'grahs'.

So how do we explain the pronunciation differences currently heard around Australia? This particular variation has existed from the beginning of settlement and is undoubtedly due to the different dialect mixes in each region. There are a number of complicating factors involved, but at least one of the reasons for the prevalence of the older 'flat a' pronunciation in Melbourne and other parts of Victoria is that a significant number of people settled there from the north of England.

At the moment it's difficult to predict what this variation will do in Australia. Which way will it go? As research by linguists Barbara Horvath and David Bradley shows, it's all become very complicated. Firstly, the vowels don't occur uniformly across all words; for example, you might find people in Melbourne saying 'castle' with the 'flat a' but 'dahns' and 'plahnt'. There are also complex social and stylistic factors involved. If you went to a private school, you're more likely to say 'dahns'. And if the situation is a more formal one, the likelihood of 'dahns' is even greater. (I don't believe it's a coincidence that onomatopoeic *la-di-da* contains this particular vowel.) As Bradley points out, the word *advance* in the last line of the national anthem 'Advance Australia Fair' is far more likely to be pronounced 'advahns' here than in other contexts – even by those who might normally find this pronunciation pretentious.

For significant dialect differences to develop, you need time. English hasn't been in Australia that long, certainly not long in terms of language change. You also need distance – physical and social distance. All languages will change, but they don't necessarily change in the same way in different places. Physical distances between Australian towns are considerable, of course. What's more, never underestimate the solidarity function of language. Regional chauvinism, as evident in the strong rivalry between places like Sydney and Melbourne, is a major incentive for people to start highlighting their distinctiveness linguistically. The *castle–cahstle* tug of war could well become one of the great divides in Australia as it has in other parts of the English-speaking world. Time will tell.

Bust versus burst

A friend of mine has a bit of a thing about the colloquial pronunciation of *burst* as 'bust'. In fact, this curious pronunciation change has gone far beyond this single pair of words, but for some reason it's *bust* that gets up his nose. He doesn't seem aware of other doublets, or at least they don't distress him in the same way: *curse* versus *cuss*, *barse* (the fish) versus *bass*, and of course *arse* versus *ass*. There were once many more of these but most have disappeared, at least from mainstream English: *horse* versus *hoss*, *nurse* versus *nuss*, *thirsty* versus *thusty* and *first* versus *fust*. Some of them are lingering a little longer in the regions. In some rural dialects, for example, you can still hear pronunciations such as *fust* and *thusty* in place of *first* and *thirsty*.

All of these words have in common an original 'r' sound appearing before 's'. The 'r' is preserved in the spelling, although no longer pronounced, at least by varieties like Standard British, Australian and New Zealand English. In these words it's assumed that the 'r' dropped out and the vowel then changed. In particular, it was shortened. But in fact, doublets like these are not confined to this group of words. They involve a much wider range of vocabulary items. Think of examples such as *baby* versus *bubby, saucy* versus *sassy, girl* versus *gal* and even *teat* versus *tit*. These are stylistic doublets that differ not just in terms of vowel quality but also in formality. All of them have in common that the first member of the doublet has a long vowel, and this is typically the standard or respectable term. Its partner, on the other hand, has a short vowel, and is the vernacular term. *Bust* is certainly more colloquial than *burst*. Indeed, many of these shortened versions belong in the realm of slang, such as *gal* and *tit*.

The shortening of vowels here is probably simply a factor of the commonness of the word. Shortcuts and reductions are a fact of lexical life when it comes to casual everyday speech. Quite simply, the repetition of words causes them to reduce. In this case the shortened form doesn't end up replacing the longer form, but both co-exist as stylistic variants. Eventually they may part company in meaning as well – *tit* is not only vulgar, it has quite a different sense from *teat*. Extreme examples are *hussy* from *housewife, stroppy* from *obstreperous* and *grotty* from *grotesque*. The more colloquial terms here show not only the characteristic short vowel but also an impressive loss of original vowels and consonants. And, of course, the meanings have diverged, too – to such an extent, in fact, that we don't even think of these as doublets any more. Few people these days would ever connect *grotty* with *grotesque* or *hussy* with *housewife*. The use of these words in casual settings has obviously not only had a profound effect on pronunciation, it has also led these words down quite a different semantic track. This has then led to the creation of two radically different words as the long and the short versions parted company.

But let me return to my friend's pet peeve: *burst* versus *bust*. To recap – stylistic doublets of this kind are widespread, and in all of them the more colloquial member (sometimes also dialectal) has a shorter vowel while its more reputable partner retains a longer vowel. Here lies the clue to a very puzzling etymology – the origin of the dreaded 'F-word'. Many of you, I feel sure, would probably prefer the origin of this word remained obscure, but I have to raise it here since so many dubious etymologies have been proposed. The most likely source for this colourful item of language is the venerable early English verb *firk*, meaning 'to strike, hit or beat'. The sexual sense would have grown out of this cluster of meanings sometime during the 16th century. It's evident, for instance, in that rather gorgeous, now archaic expression for 'foreplay' – *firkytoodling*. The metaphor here is obvious. It certainly appears behind many modern slang terms for the sex act, such as *to bang, bonk, boff, knock off* – there are a lot of them. And the vowel change that transforms ancient *firk* to the modern-day 'F-word' is, of course, well attested in the doublets just mentioned: *curse–cuss, thirsty–thusty, nurse–nuss, burst–bust, firk* …

There are a number of additional expressions that would have helped push *firk* along this path. Successful slang terms, you'll find, rarely have a single origin. Most are lexical hybrids, mixed breeds with a complex array of different sources that collide historically to form a kind of semantic network that then has the effect of establishing the meaning of the term. I'll spare you the details of the impressive semantic network supporting the English 'F-word', but let me assure you it's about as complex as you can get. This little word is one etymological mongrel.

'Skisms', 'shisms', 'sisms'?

Recently I heard an interview on radio, part of which went something like this: 'So, what do you think is causing all these schisms [pronounced 'skisms']?' asked the interviewer.

'Well', replied his guest, 'schisms [pronounced 'sisms'] like these in the Church go back a long way'.

The interviewer was Australian and his guest American. So, who is correct in this case? Is the word pronounced 'skism' or is it 'sism'? In fact, if you look up *The Macquarie Dictionary* and the *Webster's Dictionary* you'll discover a third possibility, namely 'shism'.

Australian English speakers will hate this but, from the point of view of its etymology at least, the American English speaker got it right – it's 'sism'. 'Skism' is historically a mispronunciation, as is the 'shism' that appears in *The Macquarie* and *Webster's* dictionaries. The word was originally borrowed from French. It appears to have entered English sometime during the 14th century and at that time it was normally spelt with 'sc' or 'c'. The pronunciation would most certainly have been with an initial 's' sound, in other words something like 'sism'.

The problem is, the word got respelt. There was a lot of tinkering with spelling during the Renaissance period, usually in an attempt to indicate the history of a word. Some scholars felt that if a term had a Greek or Latin pedigree this should be made obvious in its appearance. So 'sism' suddenly found itself with an initial 'sch' spelling, to make it look more respectable, more classical. And, as writing became more important in the society, so learned respellings like this one could then trigger a change in pronunciation. Hence, the word we once said as 'sism' changed its pronunciation to bring it into line with its fancy new spelling. The problem is, no one was quite sure how to pronounce it. So it received two new pronunciations, one with the 'sk' of 'skism' and the other with the 'sh' of 'shism'. And in this case, of course, 'sism' lingered on as well, leaving us with three possibilities.

Now, this word 'skism, shism, sism', however you choose to say it, isn't a very common expression, especially in speech. So the problem of how to pronounce it doesn't crop up terribly often. But there is a word that has precisely the same difficulty and it is in common usage. This is the word 'skedule' – or is that 'shedule'? Or indeed, is it even 'sedule'? The pronunciation 'skedule' tends to be American. It was the one recommended by Noah Webster in his *American Dictionary of the English Language* (1828). The Standard British pronunciation is 'shedule'. Both are in fact historically mispronunciations. The rendition truest to the word's origin is indeed 'sedule' – a pronunciation that was common in both the UK and America during the 1800s but then disappeared. Like 'sism', the word originally came into English from French during the 14th century. At that time it was spelt with an initial 's' or 'c', true to its French origin. But once again scholars tinkered with it and introduced a fashionable respelling, 'schedule', to give it a more illustrious Latin look. The historically expected pronunciation 'sedule' lingered for a while, but eventually gave way to the later spelling pronunciations 'skedule' and 'shedule'.

I'm not sure why these early scholars changed the spelling in this way. Perhaps it was linguistic snobbery. They may simply have wanted to show off their knowledge of Greek and Latin – even if they did get it wrong, which they often did. Or perhaps some of them genuinely did believe they were helping to standardize English spelling, which was notoriously irregular at that

The conservatism of American English

 It seems that every time I mention American English in this book it's in reference to some older feature of English that is preserved in this dialect but has disappeared elsewhere. Indeed, many of the linguistic features understood to be characteristically American are conservative. The English that's currently spoken in America preserves a good many features that didn't survive in British English, and consequently never made it here to Australia. (Some readers should bear this in mind next time they're slinging off at American accents in historical movies!)

But let me not give the impression that all American usage represents older English. Language change works both ways, and General American English has lost a number of features, too. Many of these are vocabulary items. Not unexpectedly, the US has no use for words describing aspects of the natural landscape such as *copse, thicket, spinney, dell, fen, moor* and *heath* – and these words no longer form a part of our active vocabulary in Australia, either. But American English has also lost some surprising words – and one is that very useful term *fortnight*.

American English has also been innovative, of course. For example, many fine English terms of Standard English today were created by Americans – including *calculate, bookstore, lengthy, antagonize, belittle* and *presidential*. I should point out, too, that in the 1700s these particular examples were described as 'barbarous' Americanisms. Outside the United States it took some time for people to realize the virtues of these linguistic weeds! And as a final note, we Australians should probably not forget that some items from our beloved Aussie lingo also have their origins in early North America. *Squatter* for example – and even that quintessentially Australian word *bush*.

time. Latin certainly had a more regular spelling, and bringing the English word into line with its supposed Latin equivalent was regularizing of a sort – helpful, perhaps, for those who had a classical education but hardly an improvement for the vast majority who didn't! For the latter group, this classy respelling simply introduced an even greater discrepancy between script and sound. For instance, the word *scissors* changed from the original and more sensible 's' or 'c' spelling to the 'sc' spelling we find today. But unlike in the case of *schism* and *schedule*, this time we didn't change our pronunciation. And so now we're left with an awkward situation where the 's' sound of *scissors* has yet another representation, this time a cluster of letters 'sc'.

There are many, many examples of this kind, where scholars were inspired by their notions of etymology to alter English spellings. Words like *debt* and *doubt*, for instance, got a 'b' simply to Latinize them. And these days such is the power of writing over speech that people now actually do maintain that *debt* and *doubt* have a silent 'b'. The truth is, this 'b' was only ever decorative. These words never had a 'b' until some bright spark inserted it sometime during the 16th century. And now we accuse the word of dropping its 'b' – once again the written tail wags the spoken dog!

Ashoom or assume?

One of the most common processes of sound change is the tendency for vowels and consonants to become like others that are nearby, in other words, assimilation. Essentially, sounds will change their shape depending on the company they keep. These sorts of changes are an inherent characteristic of casual speech. They needn't have any long-term effect, but when they do they can bring about significant changes in the actual sound system itself by creating, for example, brand new consonants as well as vowels.

A good example is the 'ch' sound that we now pronounce in words such as *chin* and *cheese*. This sound grew out of 'k'. It began life as exactly this sort of fast speech phenomenon. To see how it happens, think of the high-speed pronunciation of something like *miss you* or *fit you*. OK, in slow and careful speech you might well say 'miss you' and 'fit you', but in normal rapid speech it's much more likely that you will draw the 's' of *miss* and the 't' of *fit* towards the 'y' of 'you' and produce these something like 'mishoo' (or 'misha') and 'fitchoo' (or 'fitcha'). Sloppy speech, careless speech, you might be thinking – perhaps. But it's exactly this process that has given rise to pronunciations such as 'capcha' for *capture*, 'mishon' for *mission*, 'mezha' for *measure*, 'soldja, for *soldier* and 'righchous' for *righteous*. No one these days would think of pronouncing these as they are spelt, unless it were to sound theatrical.

The sounds that you now hear in the middle of these words are described as palatals, so-called because they involve the front of the tongue being raised towards the hard palate (basically the bony part of the roof of the mouth). They evolved through this same process of assimilation. These palatal sounds aren't natives, something we inherited from Germanic. You can tell that from the spelling. They don't have their own symbols, but are usually represented by 's', 'z', 't' and 'd'.

We know that the palatal pronunciations of these words became firmly established in the course of the 17th century. But we also know from the spellings of around that time that the changes began as early as the 15th century. Roger Lass, in his account of the history of early Modern English, gives examples such as *sessions* spelt *sesschyonys*, *obligation* as *oblygashon*, *soldier* as *sawgear* and *tedious* as *teges*.

Assimilation changes of this kind are always more likely to occur if speakers have no notion of the written word. Such changes will slow down considerably, perhaps even stop altogether, with a knowledge of spelling. Indeed, speakers dumped many of these new palatal pronunciations as soon as they started to pay attention to writing. For example, in *tedious* we've ended up restoring the original pronunciation; 'teges' (or 'tejous') now sounds odd. But there was a lot of variation around in these early times, as you'd expect. For instance, the 18th-century writer Nares notes the pronunciation 'dj' in words like *grandeur* and *soldier* but does not know if 'it is a pronunciation of which we ought to approve'. But he does accept 'ch' for *bestial, celestial, courtier* and *frontier*. 'Bestchal' and 'celestchal' probably sound fine to modern ears, but 'courcher' and 'froncher' almost certainly do not! Nares also gives 'sh' as the pronunciation for *nauseate, Persian* and *issue*, and 'zh' for *evasion, confusion* and *azure*. You can see that the pronunciations we have today show a mixture of both the new palatal sounds and the conservative spelling pronunciations.

Palatal sounds were also appearing in more obvious positions, not just hidden in the middle of words. During the 1600s, for example, people started pronouncing 'sh' at the beginning of *sue*, *suitor* and *suit*. This was occasionally reflected in spellings – *sue* as *shue*, *suiter* as *shooter* and *suit* as *shuite*. But there was a lot of resistance to these pronunciations. Cooper, writing in 1687, condemns them as 'barbarous' and most were eventually abandoned. However, a couple did manage to sneak through and survive. These are represented in our current pronunciations of the words *sure* and *sugar*.

Nowadays we attach enormous importance to writing and, more than ever before, this is affecting pronunciation by way of retarding the normal processes of change – perhaps even reversing them. Pronunciations such as 'Indjin' and 'idjit' for *Indian* and *idiot* were also once commonplace, but people were feeling increasingly queasy about them and the older pronunciations were eventually restored. As you've probably noticed, there is still substantial variation, sometimes quite a tug of war in fact, between different pronunciations. Do you prefer 'ashoom' and 'prezhoom' or 'asyum' and 'presyum' for *assume* and *presume*? Or a third possibility; namely, 'assoom' and 'prezoom' – in North America most have opted to drop the 'y' sound, which then nicely sidesteps the issue of whether or not to assimilate here.

Opus – opera

English has many examples of funny plurals. Some of these are inherited, such as *mouse–mice* and *woman–women*. Some of them are exotic. This latter group includes highfalutin plurals, classical imports from Latin or Greek such as *referendum–referenda,* and *index–indices*. Surely among the strangest of the alien plurals must be those words of Latin origin that take an *-ra* ending – *corpus–corpora* and *opus–opera*, for example. A lot of these have now disappeared, having been overtaken by that very successful English plural ending *-s*. So the plural of *corpus* has become *corpuses*, at least for most speakers. Other such words have been regularized in different ways. In the case of *opus* and *opera*, the forms have now parted company. Few would connect *opus* 'a work or composition' with *opera*, a specific (singular) kind of 'musical

Constable, money, honey, love

 There are many tricky aspects to English spelling, but one of the trickiest is the representation of vowel sounds. Let me take just one example – the letter 'o'. This has a number of different pronunciations. I'll just mention two of them. In *front* it's an 'uh' sound – and also in words such as *comfort, compass, onion* and *stomach*. In *bomb* it's a short 'oh' sound – also in *conquer, conquest, bonnet* and *combat*. But then there are words that seem to want it both ways – *constable* and *comfrey*, for example. All these words have a nasal sound following, either 'n' or an 'm'. They came into English from French, a good many of them during the 13th century – which is when we filched most of our French vocabulary. Now, in Anglo-French it's assumed they all came to be pronounced with a 'oo' sound. Then a later change shifted this sound to the 'uh' pronunciation we find today in *stomach, company, comfort* and *onion*. So far so good.

But what about words like *combat, dromedary, bonnet* and *conquer*? Why aren't they pronounced the same way as *stomach, company, comfort* and *onion*? There are two things happening here. Firstly, it might be to do with the date they entered English. Some of these came into the language late, and therefore they arrived with a different pronunciation already in tow. Secondly, the pronunciations you hear today could also be the result of a spelling pronunciation. As described earlier, if a word's spelling and pronunciation don't agree, such is the prestige of writing now that speakers may change the pronunciation to suit the spelling. The word *comrade*, for example, was originally pronounced in the same way as *company* – well into the 19th century, in fact. Then when the written word became important, people changed their pronunciation to conform to it. This accounts for the alternative pronunciations you still hear in words such as *constable, comfrey, frontier, dromedary*. There's still a tussle going on between the older pronunciation and the reintroduced spelling pronunciation.

153

drama'. But this is not what I want to focus on here. Instead, I want to look at how a language like Latin could ever have arrived at such a peculiar plural. How on earth do you get from *corpus* to *corpora*?

It's actually a pronunciation matter. It might sound odd, but it's natural to change 's' into 'r', at least when it's surrounded by vowel sounds. This is just one of the many types of weakening processes that are so much a part of sound change. The 's', when it's in the close company of vowels, gradually loses its status as a consonant and becomes more like a vowel. If you think about the pronunciation of 'r', it really is very vowel-like. For a start it's voiced, but it also has the sonorous, richly resonating quality of a vowel. (Sounds produced when the vocal cords are vibrating are said to be 'voiced', and those produced when the vocal cords are apart are said to be 'voiceless'. Lightly put your fingertips on your voice box and make an 'ah' sound. You'll be able to feel the voice by vibrations produced.)

This process, once again, is assimilation – sounds taking on the qualities of their neighbours. The vast majority of sound changes are of this kind. So common is the change that turns 's' into 'r' that it has its very own label – 'rhotacism', a word derived from the Greek name for the sound and letter 'r'. So, the plural of *corpus* would originally have been formed simply by tagging on some kind of ending. By adding this ending, the 's' suddenly found itself flanked by vowels. This triggered the changes that then turned the 's' of *corpus* into the 'r' of *corpora*.

Latin has many examples of related words where 's' alternates with 'r' in this way. Some have made it into English. Not only has *opus* given us *opera*, but also the verb *operate*. Adjectives like *oral, rural* and *floral* all derive from nouns ending in 's' – *os* 'mouth', *rus* 'open land' and *flos* 'flower'. The same change also shows up in curious pairs of words like *agnostic* and *ignorant*. Both these derive from the root meaning 'to know' (this is the 'gn' bit that shows up in the 'gnos' of *agnostic* and the 'gnor' of *ignorant*). With a bit of phonological imagination you can see the same 's'/ 'r' alternation here. The 'r' in the word *ignorant* is the result of rhotacism.

It's not just in Latin that you find this change. Rhotacism was also alive and well in early English and its close Germanic relatives. But only traces of this once lively pronunciation rule now survive in the form of linguistic fossils like *was* versus *were*. English spelling, itself being a large kind of linguistic fossil, preserves the final vowel that would have been the original trigger for turning 's' into 'r' in the verb form *were*. There are other fossils where the connection is not quite as obvious. In the word *forlorn*, for instance, the *lorn* bit is actually historically related to the verb *lose* – the 'r' in *forlorn* shows the effects of early rhotacism. Of course, there's now quite a difference between the meanings of *forlorn* and *lose*, although you can still find the link. *Forlorn* did once mean 'lost', but specifically 'lost in the mind', or 'morally lost' or 'depraved'. It's not too far-fetched to get from here to the current meanings 'forsaken' and 'miserable'.

We can also trace the historical relationship between the words *rise* and *rear* back to rhotacism. *Rear* derives from *rise*. These meanings aren't so distant. *Rear* means something like 'to cause to rise', whether it's a horse rearing up or the rearing of a child. *Sneeze* and *snore* are similarly related. *Snore* is another fall-out of rhotacism. However, these English examples have undergone additional changes that have further obscured the relationship, and only the keenest etymologist would connect them now.

So, is this more laziness on the part of speakers? Mrs Gafoops probably thinks so. Certainly sound changes such as rhotacism do make life easier for speakers – but in pronunciation only. It might be easier to pronounce 's' as 'r' when it's between vowels, but this wreaks havoc with the grammatical system, as is made evident in eccentricities of English grammar like *was* and *were*. As is so often the case in linguistic change, simplification in one area has introduced greater complexity and anomaly elsewhere. What's good for pronunciation isn't necessarily good for grammar.

Fingers don't fing

Why is it that *fingers* and *singers* have such different pronunciations? In the first word we pronounce the 'g', but not in the second. And where does the 'g' sound in the middle of *longer* come from?

It all has to do with the complicated story of that nasal consonant you hear at the end of words such as *sing* and *long*. This is a sound produced at the back of the mouth. The fleshy bit at the end of your hard palate is lowered and there's closure between it and the back of the tongue. We've always written the sound with the cluster of letters 'ng'. The earliest Germanic spelling systems did have special symbols for this sound, but our Roman-based orthography never has. In phonetics it's represented by a single symbol, ŋ, and I'll use this here because the spelling does tend to get in the way.

Originally, the sound had no special significance – it was simply a variant pronunciation of 'n'. When 'n' occurred before sounds such as 'k' and 'g' that were pronounced at the back of the mouth, the 'n' accommodated and obligingly shifted its pronunciation to the back of the mouth also. This is what happens when we say the word *pancake* – in normal rapid speech we all pronounce it as 'paŋcake'. Nasal sounds are definitely the chameleons of the phonological world – they're forever changing their colour to blend into their environment. So the word *sing* originally would have been pronounced as 'siŋg'. You can still hear this pronunciation in parts of the UK – for example, dialects spoken in the West Midlands area.

Sometime during the 16th century there was a significant sound change that affected the pronunciation of the 'g' consonant. When it occurred at the end of words and after a nasal sound, it dropped off. Hence 'siŋg' came to be pronounced as 'siŋ'. It was at this time also that 'b's were dropping off the end of words such as *lamb* and *climb*. And 'd's were dropping off as well. Our word *lawn*, for instance, once used to end in 'd' – for some reason our spelling reflects this particular change but not the others. So we're dealing here with a widespread shift that saw the loss of 'b', 'd' and 'g' when they appeared after nasals. But this change happened only when these sounds occurred at the end of a word. It's the usual story. The ends of words are always more weakly articulated, and are therefore prone to this kind of decay. Hence, 'g's that were stuck in the middle of words were protected – examples like *finger, angry, longer, hunger* and yes, as you would expect, *singer* 'one who sings'. So during this time, and I'm talking roughly about the late 16th to early 17th centuries, the word we nowadays pronounce as 'siŋiŋ' would have been pronounced 'siŋgiŋ'. Only the 'g' at the end dropped off. The one in middle was protected and therefore survived.

The question remains: if only final 'g's dropped off, what then happened to the 'g' in the middle of *singing* and *singer*? Sometime during the 1700s people started to expand the 'g'-less pronunciation to related words. It was a way of tidying things up. So the 'g' not only disappeared from *sing*, but also from the forms derived from *sing*, namely *singing* and *singer*. It disappeared from *hang* and therefore also from *hanging* and *hanger*. And so, since a *finger* is not something that 'fings', the 'g' here was preserved. (In fact, historically, *finger* is a derived form, being related to *fang*, but that was just too long ago to be relevant!)

What we are seeing in this instance is analogy at work. The 'g'-less pronunciation had been such a great hit with speakers that they extended it to other words. There were some surprises though. Certain forms managed to sneak through with their 'g'

Dropping a 'g'

When people talk about dropping a 'g' in a word such as *swimming* (in other words, pronouncing it 'swimmin'), bear in mind that this is not really dropping a 'g'. The 'g' consonant at the end of *swimming* had already dropped off nearly 500 years ago. What people are doing here is changing the nature of the final nasal. We are substituting 'n' in place of 'ŋ'. The fact that we describe this change as dropping a 'g' once again reflects the priority we now give to writing as opposed to speech. Even though speech is clearly primary, these days we tend to view it as a kind of careless and muddled version of writing. We put letters before sounds.

The curious thing about pronunciations like 'swimmin' is that they were once considered quite posh. Early pronouncing dictionaries make this clear. Cooper, for instance, writing in 1685 states that *coughing* and *coffin* are pronounced the same way: both as 'coffin'. Tennyson, Byron, Wordsworth and Keats used to rhyme these sorts of words, too. It wasn't until the end of the 1800s that we developed our dread of the so-called dropped 'g'. People then started to feel very strongly that pronunciation should reflect spelling – and if it didn't, then they would change the way they spoke.

intact. Think of how we pronounce words such as *longer* and *younger* (compared to *long* and *young*). It's curious that we still articulate the 'g' in the middle of them. If speakers dropped the 'g' in the middle of *singer* and *singing* to bring them in line with *sing*, why didn't they do the same for *longer* and *younger*? These exceptions are very common, everyday adjectives. The less usual adjectives, such as *cunning*, have fallen in line and have dropped the 'g' in the middle. Say to yourself, 'he's the cunningest fellow I know'. The 'g' has disappeared here, unlike in *youngest* or *longest*. If I were to coin a new adjective, say, *tring*, meaning 'attractively miniature', the derived forms *tringer* and *tringest* would also be regular. Once again, it's the common usage words that are exceptional. The frequency of words like *longer* and *younger* reinforces their bad behaviour and makes them stronger and more able to resist the cleaning up activities of analogy.

Pronunciation of *grown*

The Australian National Dictionary Centre, together with Oxford University Press, publish a regular newsletter called *Ozwords*. In it there are always a number of interesting letters from readers commenting on some aspect of English usage. In the November 2002 issue was a note from a reader who had been closely observing the pronunciation of words such as *shown* and *known*. The letter begins: 'I have been waiting for comment on the new trend by the 'me' generation to insert 'u' into words ending in OWN. Thus we are SHOWUN things on TV'. This person was also concerned that this trend might be spreading to similar-sounding words such as the personal name *Joan* and also words like *groan* – will we eventually be pronouncing these 'jowun' and 'growun'? It's an interesting question.

What's involved here are the past participles of a small group of verbs within the traditional class of so-called 'strong' verbs. These include all the irregular ones such as *eat–ate–eaten* and *drive–drove–driven* that indicate past time by modifying their vowels. You can guess by looking at the strong verb forms *eaten* and *driven* that 'knowun' and 'growun' don't represent a new trend at all, despite the suggestion of the reader of *Ozwords*. These are the forms you find in 10th-century Old English, and even well into the early modern period you can still find spellings like 'blowen' and 'knowun' for *blown* and *known*. These are linguistic leftovers that managed to survive in parts of Britain. They would therefore have made it into the melting pot of English dialects that travelled to the Antipodes – and they would have been here from the very beginning of settlement.

The pronunciations 'knowun' and 'growun' are still currently heard in and around Glasgow, and in Irish English too. They are also a feature of South African English. Here in the Antipodes they appear to be on the increase. Recent studies in both New Zealand and Australia strongly suggest that we will be hearing more of them in future. It seems these relic forms are reasserting themselves and making a comeback. It's not a trend that will please all. Since the 1960s people have been describing these pronunciations, both here and in New Zealand, as sloppy, wrong and downright offensive. I recall an article on this topic from the 1980s written by Max Harris – he called the piece 'Descent into Linguistic Slobdom'. However, some will be delighted by this development. I'm thinking particularly of those members of the Society for the Preservation of Old English Strong Verbs, who have campaigned long and hard for the preservation of such verb forms. They, no doubt, will be thrilled by 'knowun' and 'growun'.

So is the reader of *Ozwords* correct? Will the pronunciation spread beyond the verbs to similar-sounding words? It seems to me highly unlikely. These pronunciations still involve the past participles of only nine verbs – *blown, flown, grown, known, mown, sewn, shown, sown* and *thrown*. It would be unlikely for them to expand beyond this small class of verbs to words like *moan* and *groan*. And even given the ability of English speakers to remodel beyond recognition the personal names of others, the *Joans* and *Simones* out there probably have nothing to fear from 'Jowun' and 'Simowun'.

'Put your orthography where your head is'

There are a number of different ways you might write a language such as English. We could, for instance, have a symbol for each word. These symbols are sometimes called logograms; they are the 'characters' of languages such as Chinese and the Japanese *kanji.* Alternatively, we could pay more attention to the sounds of the language, and there are several possibilities here. Perhaps we could have a symbol for each syllable. There are plenty of languages that do this. A number of early writing system were syllabaries, and today you find them in languages such as Cherokee and Japanese (specifically, the Japanese *kana*). Or we could devise a set of symbols where each represents the separate sounds that make up a syllable. This is, of course, the alphabetic convention English speakers are most familiar with.

Many people complain that the English writing system lets us down because it's not phonetic enough. There isn't a sufficiently close relationship between script and sound. I admit there are inconsistencies, and examples are easy to find. Take the consonant sound 't'. This sound is represented by the letter 't' as in *tap,* by double 'tt' as in *butt,* 'te' in *Kate,* 'ed' as in *jumped,* 'th' as in *Thomas,* 'pt' as in *receipt,* 'bt' in *debt,* 'ct' in *victuals* – even 'phth' in the word *phthisis* (a medical term for some sort of wasting disease; not a term I use terribly often, I'll admit, but useful if you want to point out some of the absurdities of English spelling). There are in fact about twelve different ways of spelling the consonant 't' – and this is hardly ideal!

So while we want a better relationship between script and sound, certainly, we do not want the phonetic system that people often argue for. Let me explain. Take the consonant sound 't' again, this time as it appears in *ton, stun, bet* and *better.* The 't' consonant has quite different pronunciations in each of these words, depending on where it appears. At the beginning of a word like *ton* it's followed by a little puff of air (if you lit a match and said the word *ton* you'd likely blow it out). After 's' in a word like *stun* this puff of air is suppressed (you'd be uphill blowing out the match here). At the end of a word like *bet,* the 't' is almost swallowed, and in the middle of word like *better* it's pronounced more like a 'd'. These 't's are all very different sounds. A phonetic system (such as the International Phonetic Alphabet) represents each of these sounds with different symbols. We don't need these sorts of phonetic details represented in our writing because they don't make any difference to the meaning or understanding of the word. The different phonetic shapes of 't' are all predictable and are not significant. Speakers make them automatically. What we want a spelling system to capture is unexpected variation.

Respelling English words more phonetically would also mean we'd lose one of the real virtues of our writing system. Think of a group of words like *electric, electricity* and *electrician*. Here we retain the root of the word in the spelling ELECTRIC. If we were to spell these words on phonetic grounds we'd have to write a 'c' (or 'k') for *electric*, an 's' for *electricity* and 'sh' for *electrician*. In other words, we'd lose the meaning relationship between these words. Or think of *create, creature* and *creation*. Once again the meaningful root of these words is preserved, despite the addition of endings that change the pronunciation of the 't' and occasionally the vowel sound. Do we really want to spell *creature* 'creachure'? OK, this might make life easier for foreign students of English, but for native speakers this is all predictable stuff. We don't need to spell *creation* 'creashon'.

Our language is full of examples like these. Think of pairs of words like *line–lineal, insane–insanity, sign–signal*. Once again the relationship between each of the words in these pairs is preserved despite the different pronunciations. In short, ours is a spelling system that retains the shape of words. And this has great advantages. Firstly, it endures better over time. English did once have a system with a closer relationship between script and sound – and look what happened. The language went through massive sound changes, particularly in the area of vowels. The result is that thousands of words are now spelt more as they were pronounced in medieval times.

There's one thing English speakers love to do and that's point out the inconsistencies of English spelling. Someone called Zachrisson, for example, in 1931 reported that, on the basis of all possible combinations of sounds, it was possible to spell the word *scissors* 596,580 different ways. Apparently Dr Dewey took the time to figure out that *foolish* could be spelt 613,975 ways. Bernard Shaw, you might remember, was the one who suggested we could write the word *fish* as 'ghoti'. But English spelling isn't simply a defective phonetic script, as these examples suggest. Ours is a more abstract system that combines what is phonetically representative and grammatically so. This is a better representation of what native speakers carry around in their heads than a purely phonetic system. It's more psychologically real. As the American linguist Wayne O'Neil once said in defence of English spelling – 'don't put your orthography where your mouth is; put it where your head is'.

To hyphenate or not to hyphenate

There are many unpredictable aspects to English spelling, and whether to hyphenate or not is one of them. Do you eat *hot-dogs, hotdogs* or *hot dogs?* Even dictionaries don't seem to agree on the conventions they adopt. For instance, recently I found myself having to write *placename*. My gut feeling was no hyphen – *placename* as a single word. *The Macquarie Dictionary* was on my side here. But both my *Concise Oxford* and *Merriam–Webster's* wanted a hyphen between *place* and *name*. And my computer spell checker? Well, it went for the third option – *place name* as two individual words. So who's correct? Let me quote what the editors of *The Concise Oxford English Dictionary* once wrote on the matter: 'After trying hard at an early stage to arrive at some principle that should teach us when to separate, when to hyphen, and when to unite the parts of compound words, we had to abandon the attempt as hopeless, and welter in the prevailing chaos'. If the guardians of the English language have no idea, small wonder the rest of us are confused.

Much of the time it seems to boil down to personal preference, although there are general tendencies. If compounds involve single-syllable words, then we usually write them as one word, hence *icebox* and *eardrum*. The longer the string, the more inclined we are to separate the parts of the compound. We're not like our close relative German, a language renowned for the long compounded word. Clumps of English like *occupational choice-vocational interest congruency* or *young driver risk taking research* appear with hyphens or spaces. Familiarity is another factor. Brand new compounds are typically written with spaces or hyphens between the parts. But when they become more common, they start appearing as unified words. For example, *beer goggles* ('the distorted perception triggered by a larger than usual consumption of alcohol') is a very recent addition to the English language. It's usually written with a space and occasionally with a hyphen. Should the word be successful, the space or hyphen will probably be abandoned. Those who frequently don beer goggles have probably already done so.

Familiarity is also a factor in those situations when we use the hyphen in complex words like *re-iterate*. Many prefer hyphens here, especially where the prefix ends in the same letter as the beginning of the word it precedes, such as *anti-intellectual*, or where a solid word might suggest a single syllable, as in *co-ordinate*. But even so, when these words become commonplace we usually abandon the hyphen. Words like *coeducation* and *cooperate* have lost their hyphen, despite the potential confusion of having the two vowels together. The removal of hyphens is actually part of a more general process of integration. Well-aged compounds will over time see their component parts become more and more closely associated until the boundaries between them are completely obliterated. Eventually nothing will remain of the original compound. Just look at what's happened to the pronunciation of *boatswain*. The spelling preserves the original compound, but the pronunciation 'bosun' shows *boat* and *swain* completely fused. The longer the compound has been around, the more extreme the fusion. Think of words such as *daisy* from the compound *day's eye*, *window* from *wind eye* and *lord* from *loaf warden*.

When it comes down to it, hyphens are totally dispensable in established compounds and my feeling is we'd be better off without them. This would then free up this piece of punctuation for the much more useful task of signalling links between items where ambiguity exists. For instance, to show the difference between something like a *third-world conflict* and a *third world-conflict*. In speech, of course, there's no confusion, because intonation, stress and pausing distinguish pairs like these. But in writing, the hyphen can be used to show which items are meant to be linked – in a *third-world conflict* the hyphen between *third* and *world* indicates that we are dealing with a conflict among what are euphemistically referred to as developing or fledgling nations. A *third world-conflict* indicates a worldwide conflict happening for the third time.

But I'm a tad 'trepidacious' about suggesting we abandon the hyphen. I still recall the furious letters and emails that followed my suggestion that the possessive apostrophe was a useless addition to the English language and we should abandon it. But perhaps people aren't as passionate about the hyphen? Are there any hyphen support groups out there, I wonder? I feel sure I'll find out.

The Truly Nasty Weeds of the English Language?

The nastiest of all weeds is that sycophant – Dock, called also Herb Patience. When you grasp the strong-smelling stalk it has no fibre, it melts away in a soft squash, leaving its root in the ground; even Nettles are pleasanter to touch.
Anna Lea Merritt *An Artist's Garden* 1908

At the beginning of this book I pointed out what I thought was a problem with my use of weed imagery. Clearly there are noxious plants out there in weed flora that inflict (sometimes irreversible) damage on their environment. Linguistic weeds, I suggested, are pesky but never truly pernicious in this way. In fact, linguists would argue they are an essential part of any thriving language. But perhaps not all linguistic weeds are quite so harmless. I'm thinking in this case of aspects of language that have to do with manipulation through advertising and propaganda, of the influence of language on our thinking and behaviour, of linguistic discrimination and, in particular, of official obfuscation and games of status and power. In this next section I want to expose what look to be some really nasty weeds in our language.

The mind and language – mental illness

Dwight Bolinger, in his book *Aspects of Language*, describes language as being rather like a pair of spectacles through which we view the world. The problem is, of course, that these particular specs aren't made of clear glass. The lenses that stand between us and the world are well and truly coloured by the tinges and tints of our predilections and prejudices. Moreover, these tinges and tints are what also help to support and maintain the predilections and prejudices – the 'motes' and 'beams' in our eyes, if you like.

As an example, consider the language we use to describe mental illness and the mentally ill. *Crazy* (hence also *crazed* and *cracked*) originally meant 'flawed, damaged' (compare *crazy paving*). It both reflects and perpetuates the view that there exists a deficiency in people with mental illness, some sort of weakness or flaw in their character. This is the basis of many of our colloquial expressions for insanity: *crack-brained, scatter-brained, falling to pieces, unhinged, having a screw/tile/slate loose, not the full load, one brick short of a load, a shingle short, a sandwich short of a picnic, not playing with the full deck, two bob short of a quid, not the full quid, not playing with a full deck, three cards short of a full deck, his elevator doesn't go to the top* and so on. Many expressions are associated with the amusing: *funny (in the head), funny farm, wacky, wacko, bats, nuts, loony, nutcase, bonkers* – there are many more. The loss of control that is a feature of both slapstick humour and insanity is also evident in the different meanings of the terms *mad* and *crazy* in normal non-clinical usage. There is a long history to the perceived link between madness and funny behaviour. Recall that people once visited insane asylums for entertainment – with an entry fee of one penny, Bedlam had an astonishing revenue of about £400 per annum in the early 18th century!

Such is the stigma surrounding mental illness that any euphemism for the condition will quickly degenerate into a taboo term. This gives rise to a kind of lexical treadmill effect. If society's prejudiced perceptions continue to bubble away, eventually the euphemistic value will be undermined and the negative connotations will reattach themselves – and then a new euphemism must be found. During the controversy surrounding British Mencap's refusal to change the name *mental handicap*, their director of marketing observed: 'It is only a matter of time before even the most right-on expression becomes a term of abuse. It has been the same since people talked about village idiots, and "learning difficulties" is no exception. Children are already calling each other LDs as an insult' (cited in Crystal 1995, p. 177).

Mental illness has an impressive chain of euphemistic substitutions, and examples of this kind of deterioration are easy to find. The word *insanity* derives from Latin *in-* 'not' + *sanus* 'healthy'.

Now confined to 'mentally unsound', it originally had a much broader domain encompassing all bodily organs and their functions. Today even the word *sane* has narrowed under the influence of *insane* to designate a mental condition only. *Crazy* was once applicable to all manner of illness, but is now confined to mental illness alone.

The history of the word *deranged* illustrates a typical path of development for euphemisms. Originally from a verb meaning 'to disturb, disarrange', it could be qualified with the modifier *mental* to refer to people who were 'disturbed in the mind'. But once it was used in the context of mental illness, the word soon became contaminated and now, without the modifier, has narrowed to the 'mad' sense alone. Even the adjective *mental* has been affected – dictionaries still list 'pertaining to the mind' as its central sense, but 'denoting a disorder of the mind' is always given as a secondary meaning, as are the colloquial senses 'mad' and 'foolish' (compare *be/go mental*, and *become a mental patient*). It may well be that *disordered* and *afflicted* are moving in the same direction. Though still requiring a modifier like *mentally* to refer specifically to psychiatric illness, this is now becoming their normal context of use. And while dictionaries still define *sick* as 'affected by any disorder of health', in slang usage the word has narrowed to mean 'mental ill health', frequently with overtones of 'perversion' (compare *sicko* and American slang *sicknik*).

There are many more examples, including the names for establishments holding mentally ill people. These show the same rapid pejoration and restriction of meaning. A striking illustration is *asylum*. In Latin the word meant 'place of refuge, retreat', a sense still retained in *political asylum*. At first the name appears to have been used of institutions for debtors and criminals, but was later broadened to include shelters for the orphaned, the blind, the deaf and also the mad – when it required some sort of qualifier such as *lunatic*. These days the ordinary understanding of *asylum*, at least in reference to a building, is now specifically 'institution for the care of the insane'.

Western society may no longer believe in a demonological concept of mental illness, but our linguistic behaviour towards the mentally afflicted reveals the same attitudes of compounded fear and contempt. It has required a considerable rejigging of our thinking to persuade us to accept mental illness as an illness like any other – as one that can be treated. Mind you, current-day colloquial expressions for 'mentally ill' and the recent narrowing and pejoration of words such as *sick* and *afflicted* suggest our attitudes are still firmly tied to old-fashioned notions of behavioural deviance. While it is perfectly acceptable to be physically ill, it is still not quite acceptable to be mentally ill.

PC language

The political correctness debate in the 1980s and 1990s certainly did a good job of exposing some of the in-built biases of the English language, particularly in the area of vocabulary. In the tricky matter of ensuring a fair go for all, we have been made aware of many of the colours and tints of our linguistic spectacles – the hidden warps and imbalances that exist in some of our everyday expressions that are now dubbed sexist, racist, religionist, ageist and so on. I have never been convinced that getting people to alter their linguistic habits will alter their ways of thinking and behaving, but when our attention is drawn to language in this way we are forced to sit up and take notice, and this is a good thing.

A lot of PC language is meant to stick out like a sore thumb and catch the eye (or the ear). It's a form of public action. Take, for example, the use of the so-called 'generic' *she*. Recently, I've been reading a number of survival guides for parents with babies and toddlers. Even though most of these books use 'generic' *she*, I'm still taken aback when I encounter such sentences as: 'By twelve months your baby will be sitting on her own; she will probably be crawling'. The language here is, of course, intentionally distracting – it's meant to jar. Similarly, the use of *he/she* and *him/her* is meant, by some writers at least, to be deliberately clumsy: 'By twelve months your baby will be sitting on his/her own; he/she will probably be crawling'. The offence of a distracting style can be a very effective way of getting a message across.

PC language is deliberately throwing down the gauntlet and daring us to go beyond the content of the message and acknowledge the sexist principles on which our language has been operating. I see it as a kind of 'in-your-face' euphemism – euphemism that aims not to disguise or conceal unpleasant realities, but to compel its audience to challenge assumptions that some assume are in-built and immutable aspects of our language.

Those who 'misspeak' themselves

If Bob Haldeman or John Ehrlichman or even Richard Nixon had said to me, 'John, I want you to do a little crime for me. I want you to obstruct justice,' I would have told him he was crazy and disappeared from sight. No one thought about the Watergate coverup in those terms – at first, anyway. Rather it was 'containing' Watergate or keeping the defendants 'on the reservation' or coming up with the right public relations 'scenario' and the like.

John W Dean III *New York Times* 6 April 1975

The colouring of our linguistic lenses is often quite unconscious, of course – but not always. Sometimes it's very deliberate and the motives quite malign. In 19th-century Australia, *disperse* used to be an officially sanctioned euphemism for 'kill' in the context of Aboriginal killings by the 'native' police force set up in 1848. Bruce Elder describes an incident where a young subaltern, new to the police, used the word *killed* instead of *dispersed* in a report he had submitted. He was severely reprimanded for his carelessness and told to correct his error. The sub rewrote the report thus: 'We successfully surrounded the said party of aborigines and dispersed fifteen, the remainder, some half dozen, succeeded in escaping'(!). Another common euphemism was *collision* – 'collisions' between Aborigines and the police force invariably denoted killings or, as they were officially described, 'dispersals'.

I still recall the news broadcast from 1986 where reference was made to the remains of those killed in the *Challenger* space shuttle disaster as *recovered components*. This horrible piece of dehumanizing bureaucratic terminology was intended to play down a loss of human life caused by an inattention to safety measures that was motivated by short-term political and financial gain. There is no doubt in my mind that using such 'deodorant' language to describe dirty deeds makes it easier to commit those dirty deeds. Expressions like *soft skin target*, *surgical strikes*, *collateral damage* and *friendly fire* help to minimize feelings of responsibility. They play down the slaughter of human beings and also create psychological distance between the perpetrators and their actions.

It's unlikely anyone is completely taken in by such examples at the time – public opinion is not as easily manipulated as George Orwell's Newspeak would suggest. Mind you, there is plenty of evidence to show that loaded language does work to influence memory and perception. Research carried out by Elizabeth Loftus, for example, shows that the simple phrasing of a question can have a substantial effect on the testimony of an eyewitness. It may even alter how the person remembers an event. One well-known experiment involved a hundred people who were shown a film of a multiple-car crash. Fifty were asked how fast the cars were going when they 'hit'; fifty were asked how fast were they going when they 'smashed'. The second fifty averaged an estimated speed that was faster than the first fifty. Some of them also saw broken glass. Apparently there was none. Moreover, a question phrased, 'Did you see the broken headlight?' was more likely to produce false recognition or 'don't know' responses than the question 'Did you see a broken headlight?'

Words and expressions can be misleading in a very obvious way. But it's not just suasive vocabulary we have to guard against. What about structural patterns, those aspects of our language that are more than skin deep? This is persuasion at a much more subtle level. Just the simple structure of questions asked to interrogate witnesses can influence their answers. For example, if you ask a witness, 'You did see broken glass, didn't you?' this tag question is much more likely to produce a 'yes' response than a straight-forward question framed 'Did you see broken glass?' Even more worrying is that the new information introduced by this type of questioning may become indistinguishable from the facts acquired when the person actually witnessed the event – suddenly, broken glass is incorporated into the person's memory of that car crash.

Some speakers are very good at employing the hidden bias of grammar. Earlier in this book I mentioned agentless passives. These allow us to omit elements of information that would have to be stated in the active version. I could say *I decided to close down the school*, but if I wanted to downplay my involvement in the event a better phrasing would be *It was decided to close down the school*. This allows me to omit any reference to myself. It also sets up the impression that a consensus was reached, which is, of course, quite bogus. Moreover, the impersonal style lends the statement a kind of sham authority, presumably because it's reminiscent of those prestigious jargons that come to us from the sciences.

English also has the ability to package whole clauses into single noun phrases. To continue with the example above, I could turn the verb *decide* into the noun *decision*. Verbs need subjects and sometimes also objects – 'X decides Y' (where Y is some kind of clause). By using a noun like *decision* I can omit 'X' and 'Y'. In this instance, I can remove not only reference to myself, but also the unpopular action of closing down the school – *a decision has been made*. Throw in a few impressive Graeco-Latinate bits and pieces and the wording becomes even more authoritative. The school is now *scheduled for discontinuance*. This nouny style gives speakers and writers the opportunity of being non-committal as to who is doing what to whom – a sneaky device and one eminently suited to contexts where it is desirable to conceal information of this nature. A style that is heavy with nouns also adds to the general density of the language and introduces more abstractness. It's harder to follow. Turning a whole clause into a noun might be economical, but there's plenty of psycholinguistic evidence that 'nominalisations' (as they're called) present significant processing problems for hearers and readers – they make for difficult communication. It's one more bewildering aspect of the super-literate varieties we suffer today – the so-called *-eses* such as Legalese, Bureaucratese and Linguisticalese.

Discombobulation

Another earmark that distinguishes *-eses* like Bureaucratese from 'ordinary' usage is long-windedness, in particular their predilection for compounding. I'm sure you are all too familiar with the sort of prose that is clogged with congealed clumps of nouns such as *backlog reduction objects* and *case input volumes*. Usually we create compounds to fill gaps in our vocabulary, but with this kind of compounding I sometimes get the feeling that the reverse process is going on. It's as if speakers deliberately take a perfectly fine ordinary little word such as *pothole* and *door* and unpack it. Each of the senses is listed and the result is an impressive-sounding compound. *Pothole* becomes *pavement deficiency*, *door* becomes *entry system*. It's no longer *garbage* but *post-consumer secondary material*. I recall when the Australian dollar was taking a tumble in the 1980s. Dealers and economists talked of it as having a *substantial downside risk potential*.

Of course, this roundabout expression can be driven by a desire not to offend. In certain contexts you can imagine a speaker might prefer using the long-winded phrase *excrementitious human kidney fluid* rather than *urine*. For many years newspapers referred to *criminal sexual assault* rather than *rape*. I once heard someone describe 'educationally challenged groups' as *those at the lower end of the ability scale*. This person might also have said *low-ability subjects*. In this era of egalitarianism and equal opportunity for all, Educationalese has sought to abandon value-laden terms like *lazy, idle, clever* and *poor* and replace them with expressions like *educationally and socially disadvantaged groups, high verbal-ability groups, disadvantaged home environments* and *underprivileged children*. Such verbosity seems to be aimed at obscuring the differences between the educationally successful and educationally unsuccessful child (in other words, *the exceptional child*).

But then there are examples that are more dishonest – where euphemistic circumlocution is used not so much to avoid offense as to deliberately mystify the topic and to deceive. Sometimes those engaged in healthcare do make fatal mistakes and when they do they might seek to conceal the error (and save their tails). In the *Medical Observer* of 19 January 1990 is a report from

Professor William Lutz of Rutgers University. He collected the following examples of doublespeak from hospital records: *therapeutic misadventure, diagnostic misadventure of the highest magnitude, negative patient-care outcome* and *patient failed to fulfil his wellness potential.* I wondered at first whether these might be satirical inventions (much like those celebrated examples of PC-speak – the *person with hard-to-meet needs* for 'serial killers' or the *differently pleasured* for 'sado-masochists'). But Lutz has always claimed his examples are genuine. This is the language that turns *war* into *violent peace, failure* into *incomplete success, death* into *terminal living,* and *lies* into *terminological inexactitudes* and *categorical inaccuracies.*

Sometimes this discombobulation (I do love this word) looks to be pure puffed up jargon. I can understand why in a serious piece of academic writing a child psychologist might not want to talk about *hitting a naughty child* – but do they really need to go as far as *punitive external controls* (to which the child then provides *sensory feedback* rather than yells)? Somehow the jargon here seems all the more offensive because it deals with the everyday. And in this respect linguists (who after all write about everyone's language) are some of the worst offenders. Here's something my colleague Keith Allan and I once wrote about the nature of jargon: 'Since X-phemisms by definition have cross-varietal synonyms, there are alternatives to X-phemisms available; but jargon is necessary to frame a message because there really is no viable alternative; (i.e. there are no reasonably simple cross-varietal synonyms available'. Now, if this were quantum mechanics and not linguistics, probably no one would question the right to furnish the discipline with this sort of technical vocabulary. But to the non-linguist such practice seems unnecessarily pedantic and baffling. The technical language is perceived as intellectual hocus-pocus, and all the more offensive because of the everyday nature of the subject matter. It was probably examples like ours that drove Laurence Urdang, editor of *Verbatim,* to once describe my discipline as 'the pointy-headed abstruse strudel of academic linguistics' and those in the profession as 'categorically the dullest people on the face of the earth' (*The Washington Post,* 13 January 1992, p. D5) – but it does seem a little harsh!

The grammar of puff

Whatever is common is despised. Advertisements
are now so numerous that they are very negligently
perused, and it is therefore become necessary to gain
attention by magnificence of promises, and by eloquence
sometimes sublime and sometimes pathetic.
Promise, large Promise is the soul of
an Advertisement.
Dr Samuel Johnson *Idler* 20 January 1761

Certainly advertisers are keenly aware that language has the power to influence our thinking. Examples are easy to find. I remember reading once about *horse mackerel*. This was a large fish, easy to catch and simple to process. But, it seems, no one would eat it – that is, until it was renamed *tuna*. *Tuna* apparently tastes better than *horse mackerel*. University departments are very much into this kind of renaming. This year my own department changed the name of its first year unit from 'Language in Australian Society' to 'The Language Game: Why do we speak the way we do?' We've almost doubled our enrolments. So obviously advertisers will want to use the sweetest sounding words to highlight the qualities of a product (or to conceal its faults). A word such as *crafted* sounds so much better than *made* or *manufactured*. *Crafted* gives the impression that something has been produced meticulously and probably by hand. *Blend* is so much classier than *mixture*, *standard* so much better than *average*. Dressing up the goods with verbal glitz is an important part of the 'large Promise' of modern advertising.

In Samuel Johnson's day there was a word that said it all – *puff*. When it first appeared back in the 13th century *puff* referred quite simply to blasts of breath or wind, but then was extended to include anything empty or unsubstantial, particularly if it involved bragging or bluffing. By the early 17th century it had become a buzz word to describe, as *The Oxford English Dictionary* puts it, 'undue or inflated praise or commendation, uttered or written in order to influence public estimation'. A wonderful early occurrence of this meaning was a reference in 1602 to the extravagant laudation of a sugary fawner or 'puffer'

– 'Blowne up with the flattering puffes Of spungy sycophants' was the description. Puff was the hype or spin of early Modern English, and was often used to describe advertisements of the day.

It's the grammar supporting advertising *puffery* that interests me particularly. Here we're dealing with the 'deep grooves of language', as Edward Sapir once described them, and a level of persuasion that is far less obvious and very much more wily. In *Blooming English* I gave various examples of constructions that advertisers can exploit in order to be able to leave out undesirable information. One grammatical aspect I didn't mention was the nature of the verbs – in particular, their scarcity!

A lot of advertising is written in what can only be described as minced English – short sentences and sentence fragments. They're easier to understand, of course, but they also carry greater emphasis. As Dwight Bolinger points out in his book *Language: the Loaded Weapon*, the message comes across louder and clearer. Instead of 'New Sara Lee rich and creamy lite ice-cream is deliciously simple', the ad reads: 'New Sara Lee rich and creamy lite ice-cream. Deliciously simple.' What is missing here is the verb. If you get rid of verbs, your message is made without the possibility of question or doubt. The first version simply invites us to challenge it – '*Is* new Sara Lee rich and creamy lite ice-cream deliciously simple'?

But not only are there few verbs in advertisements, those that are there are very dull indeed. Believe me, I know – I once spent an entire weekend counting them. Specifically I looked at the language of food and wine advertisements in various magazines such as *New Idea* and *Women's Weekly*. The top ten on my list of verbs (a rather short list compared to nouns and adjectives) were *be, make, use, try, add, enjoy, have, help, eat, take*. Not much in the way of lexical excitement there – just a lot of dreary little verbs with very general meanings. They bring nothing to the force of the advertisement – everything goes into the nouns and adjectives that are piled on top. It's interesting to note that the majority of these verbs come from our core Germanic vocabulary. Sentences in Adspeak have in common a basic English underlay which supports a kind of lexical superstructure of largely French and Classical vocabulary. It's

175

these latter words that provide all the colour, excitement, refinement and nuance.

I shouldn't go overboard in throwing the book at advertising. After all, there can never be a neutral language, one that merely replicates or describes reality. Language itself always gets in the way. By its very nature, it will be suasive, influential, suggestive, insinuating. Whether it's advertisers, politicians – even linguists trying to persuade their readers – these writers and speakers will be guilty of embellishing their information just by the expressions and constructions they choose.

Visual euphemisms

 We've just considered examples, from food and wine advertising, of language that disguises and inflates. This is, of course, a type of euphemism. Euphemism can have many functions. It shields us against what's feared, what's disliked, what's unpleasant, what's embarrassing. But it is also used to dress up goods – to talk them up, make them more appetizing. But what about visual euphemism? So much food and drink advertising these days is accompanied by beautiful photography, by gorgeous images of the items being promoted – and often, of course, gorgeous images of things whose connection with the products is quite remote. We are all too familar with those luscious, lascivious figures used to sell cars, ice-cream, alcohol – even spaghetti sauce. When it comes to selling products, especially food products, nothing beats sex.

It's all dishonest, of course. But so is any euphemism. Think about it – in a given context, something that is taboo can be acceptably spoken of using a euphemism, but not a direct term. It's mysterious why euphemistic expressions such as *pass away, misappropriate, I'm going to the bathroom* have fewer unpleasant connotations than their corresponding taboo terms *die, steal, I'm going for a piss*. There's a very special kind of human doublethink going on here. Nonetheless, when euphemism is not driven by fear or distaste, you have to question its

176

motives. There is no doubt that some euphemism adds dimensions of deception and secrecy. And in the case of the visual euphemism the illusion is very effective. It's always much harder to prove misrepresentation when a claim is expressed non-verbally; in other words, not in propositional language with actual nouns and verbs. The visual euphemism can be a lot more sneaky.

Pleasing packaging is a type of visual euphemism. Emphasis is on appearance, not on product. Special lighting effects that redden meat, the waxing of fruit, pretty containers – these are all cosmetic, and like their verbal counterparts they create a positive illusion. They say, I'm tasty, I'm tender, I'm creamy, I'm juicy, I'm bigger than I really am. And what about the decrease in size of chocolate bars over the years? Sometimes the familiar packaging is kept, but now with *two choccy bars for the price of one*. Mind you, I'm never convinced the two together quite make up the weight of the old one. But perhaps I shouldn't be eating chocolate bars.

The taboos of today are, of course, food high in calories, carbohydrates, cholesterol, sugar, salt, caffeine. Foods are now advertised as having low quantities of these shocking substances. Slices of ham are declared to be 95 per cent fat-free. I've even heard of mineral waters that proudly proclaim on their labels: 0 calories, 0 carbohydrates, 0 fat and 0 sodium. And have you noticed those shapely, slender-waisted bottles of low-calorie salad dressing? Diet this. Lite that. The cleverly altered spelling and reversed colouring on the packaging of these products – well, they *look* non-fattening. The spelling 'l-i-t-e' looks 'light'! Still photography, film and television: these are superb media for deceptive euphemism, presenting us with a world of perfected forms where there's temptation in the chocolate bar, romance in the pasta sauce, intrigue and seduction in the cup of instant coffee, poetry in the 'hand-crafted' potato chip.

It's difficult not to look back with nostalgia to earlier times. It all seemed so honest back then. But don't get too sentimental. We've been meddling with the appearance of foods for a long, long time. In her book *Food in History*, Reah Tannahill describes some shocking practices. Apparently, in the early Middle Ages when meat was sold by piece rather than by weight, merchants had all sort of tricks up their sleeve – for example, inflating meat by blowing air through the membranes, plumping kidneys by stuffing them with rags (and not always clean ones), even sewing layers of fat onto lean meat. (What a contrast to modern times – our hankering for lean meat now leads to metabolic meddling with food animals to reduce their body fat!) In the 18th century the green of pickles could be enhanced by copper, the orange rind of Gloucester cheese by red lead. So don't get too sentimental about the old-time grocer who displayed his goods in bulk. The cosmetics of food has been going on for centuries and supporting it all the time is euphemism – verbal and visual.

How much are we led by the nose?

If our language acts as a pair of glasses with tinted lenses, can we go one step further? Are these lenses actually distorting? Does our language predispose us to a particular line of thinking and warp our view of reality? Do the differences, therefore, that exist between languages in their grammatical structure or in their vocabulary actually control our patterns of thought? As some linguists have asked: How different would Aristotle's logic have been if he had spoken Mandarin or Hopi?

The nature of the relationship between language, thought and reality has always been a hot topic. What got people really thinking about it was the work of an American named Benjamin Lee Whorf. Whorf came to linguistics from a background in fire insurance. It was petrol drums that attracted him initially to issues about language. He noted that workers were scrupulously careful with drums that were full of petrol and took an extremely casual attitude towards empty petrol drums. This is, of course, not a rational way to act, given that throwing a match into a full petrol drum will simply cause the petrol to burn, but throwing it into an empty drum will cause the petrol vapours to explode. Whorf surmised that there was something about the word *empty* that triggered the illogical behaviour of these workmen. Intrigued by this, he took up the study of language, in particular North American–Indian languages with structures and vocabularies significantly different from English. His studies led him to the notion that language actually works as a kind of filter on reality; in other words, people who speak different languages have different world views.

Let me describe a striking instance of the sort of structural difference that so impressed Benjamin Whorf. I remember, too, as a beginning student of linguistics, being bowled over when I first encountered this same illustration in Dan Slobin's textbook on psycholinguistics. The example, originally given by Whorf's teacher Edward Sapir, shows the different ways that languages express the very simple impression of a stone falling. In English we have to specify whether we're talking about one stone or several. We have to specify when this event took place, and also whether we have a specific stone in mind or just any old stone. Thus we would typically say 'The stone falls'. To us this seems a pretty reasonable way to report this event. Not so to a Russian speaker, who would find curious our attention to definiteness – 'Stone falls' is good enough. But not good enough for a German or French speaker, who has to assign the stone a gender category (in German the stone is masculine and in French feminine). Now, a Chippewa speaker would also have to include the fact that the stone is inanimate. A Kwakiutl speaker would go further and specify whether the stone is visible or invisible to the speaker at the moment of speaking, and whether it's located nearest the speaker, the hearer or some third party. Mind-boggling detail for speakers of English! But remember that we have to state that the stone is singular; Kwakiutl speakers don't. Their version could apply equally to one or several stones. And they also don't need to specify the time of the fall either, which we do via a marker on the verb.

Now, so far the event of the stone falling has been analysed by all speakers as involving two concrete notions: that of the stone and that of the action of falling. This is not how Nootka speakers would analyse it, however. They would capture the whole event in a single verb form, but one nothing like our verb *fall*. The Nootka verb consists of two main elements, the first showing the movement or position of some stone-like object, the second referring to a downward direction. Sapir gives the example of a hypothetical English verb 'to stone down'. Our sentence 'The stone falls' would be then rendered something like 'It-stones-down' (but bear in mind this is all one word in Nootka, not three as in English).

Consider another example, of which many of you will have had first-hand experience. It comes from European languages such as French or German. These languages, like many others, have a distinction between a formal 'you' pronoun and an informal 'you' pronoun. This means French and German speakers must pay special attention to questions of status and solidarity when they address someone. Every time they need to say 'you' they must make a sometimes excruciatingly difficult decision as to which one to use. Now, it's reasonable to assume that French and German speakers would therefore be much more attuned to social details to do with age, sex, status, degree of familiarity of people they are speaking to – much more than, say, English speakers who don't have to make this tricky distinction (at least not any more – remember, English did once have a formal *ye* and an informal *thou*, but the feature disappeared). It would be reasonable to assume that grammatical distinctions like this one must sensitize speakers to different aspects of the world.

But we don't want to go overboard with the notion that language controls our view of reality. Whorf's position (at least as it has been interpreted) was always a bit over the top. It is, after all, possible to speak about anything in any language, which presumably wouldn't be the case if we strictly followed Whorf's line of thinking. Languages don't differ as to what they can express – they only differ with respect to what they express more easily. This might influence our way of seeing things, but not determine it. We have in this case a pair of tinted spectacles that probably does predispose us towards acting and thinking in one way or another, but most certainly doesn't control our thoughts and behaviour patterns.

Weed control

 There isn't enough debate about language. Dwight Bolinger was right – it should be as natural to comment on the linguistic probity of advertisers, courts, businesses and offices as it is to comment on their financial probity. But it isn't.

We all need to pay more attention to the way language affects our lives – especially when it tries to lead us by the nose. Sure, there are editors who have a keen eye for the ill-chosen word, the grammatical error, the infelicities of style and punctuation. There is no shortage of gate-keepers of the language who write manuals of correct usage listing linguistic crimes from A to Z. There are countless arbiters of linguistic goodness who worry about declining standards – the Emily Post or the June Dally Watkins of linguistic etiquette. Indeed, as linguist Deborah Cameron argues, verbal hygiene is as fundamental to our linguistic competence as vowels and consonants. The problem is many seem more concerned about a dropped 'l' in *vulnerable* or an aberrant apostrophe than about attending to the real weeds of our language – or rather, language use. After all, making mistakes, lying, cheating and behaving unethically are natural human phenomena. It's language users who plant these weeds.

W(h)ither Our Weeds?

The best ground bears weeds as well as flowers.
Anonymous

Weedy plants can damage our gardens and they're sometimes
unsightly. More seriously, they can poison and injure livestock,
contaminate produce, reduce crop yields, cut down on the pro-
ductivity of pastures, choke out native species and clog up water-
ways. But the very same species can flourish attractively in
wasteland areas and urban squalor. In some rural settings they
can prevent the erosion of fragile soils in times of drought, serve
as valuable fodder plants, supply nectar for honey production,
enrich soils when rotted down, remove pollutants from domes-
tic and industrial effluent and provide a much needed habitat for
wetland wildlife. Clearly, weeds aren't intrinsically 'useless, trou-
blesome, or noxious', to quote *The Macquarie Dictionary*, and
their status changes according to local conditions. Essentially, if
a plant becomes bothersome to us, then it is defined as a weed.
In fact, some weed books suggest that every plant has a weed
inside it, and given the right set of circumstances this weed will
flourish.

And so it is with the weeds in our language. One speaker's
noxious weed can be another's cherished ornamental plant. A linguistic weed today can be a valued garden contributor tomorrow.
Whether they are in gardens or in languages, weeds are centred
around human value judgements. And they hold a real fascination for us – as Ursula Buchan describes in her book, *The Plea-
sures of Gardening*, 'like an enemy who occupies our thoughts
and schemes so much more than any friend'. Millions of dollars
are spent each year battling weeds by physical removal (hand-
pulling, hoeing, mulching) and chemical and biological controls

182

(herbicides, natural predators). Certainly, a lot of time and energy is also expended in waging weed-removal wars in our language.

Yet, when it comes to actually managing linguistic weeds, history shows quite clearly that weed-control legislation and containment programs have a dismal track record of success. For a start, our language is full of vagueness and variability, and this fuzziness makes any linguistic legislation difficult to enforce. Besides, speakers generally dislike changing their linguistic habits, and they are particularly resistant if it involves outside intervention. Basically, people don't like being told how to behave when it comes to their language. But it also seems to me that, as much as we like to complain about them, we would also miss our weeds if they disappeared. They give us a lot of pleasure – and they have their uses. Think of those awkward social occasions when we gratefully enlist the service of the weedy clichés we normally condemn. There is always something healthy about weedy language or quite simply it wouldn't grow as well as it does.

OK, you're probably thinking, what about the nasty weeds described in the previous chapter? It's true advertisers and politicians often twist and warp language, sometimes outrageously, to sell their products or to persuade their audiences. But isn't this what we all do – bend language for our own ends? The words and constructions we choose will always hint, suggest and insinuate. They never simply ditto reality. By its very nature, language has spin. Besides, there are many occasions where we don't want precise language, or even honest language, for that matter. Social interaction generally operates with the idea of harmony in mind, with a strong preference for agreement and compromise – it's generally non-hostile. We are expected to turn a tactful blind eye, perhaps, or tell a white lie. What would life be like if we exactly stated our thoughts, and in the plainest and most explicit terms? Naive communication, where speakers say literally all that is on their mind and an audience takes everything they say at face value, would be intolerable. Humans are social animals, and concerns of face are extremely important. Without these weedy tendencies in language, societal interaction would soon grind to a halt.

Clearly, a thriving language, one that caters fully for the needs of all its speakers, has to be weed-ridden. Imagine the 'perfect' linguistic system – a totally consistent, uniform, logical, transparent, neutral language, one that completely meshes with reality and is totally weed-free. Now imagine this perfect system as the first language of a group of speakers. It wouldn't take long before the weeds appeared. The facts of our existence are simply not that clear-cut. They're messy, and language has to reflect this.

There is no doubt that these weeds can be a nuisance, but it would be neither beneficial nor possible to eradicate them. Speech communities are very complex things and language must be able to reflect a vast range of social behaviour. Get rid of the weeds and the soil becomes impoverished. To steal a phrase from Mary Ellis' book on herbs, these are indeed 'virtuous weeds'.

Fulfilling the promise made earlier

To fulfil my earlier promise, let me now reveal to you the third word in the English language that ends in -*shion*. There's *cushion*. There's *fashion*. And there's at least one other. In fact, there are a number of possibilities, though none of them terribly usual words. I have to 'fess up to having help here – the Oxford Dictionaries' team and their lovely little book *Questions of English*.

The first of these words is *hushion*, a Scottish dialect word for a sort of stocking without feet – an early form of the modern-day leg warmer. As you might suspect, it's a distant relative of the word *hose* meaning 'stocking'. But unless leg warmers or footless tights make a comeback I can't imagine *hushion* really taking off. Another -*shion* word that I can pass onto you is *parishion*. It has the same meaning as *parishioner*, namely 'one of the community of a parish', but it predates *parishioner* by more than two hundred years. It was around in the early 1200s, but never seems to have gained much popularity and eventually dropped out sometime during the 16th century.

A more useful -*shion* word is *fushion*, a word meaning 'gumption', 'vigour', 'vitality' – or 'wholesomeness' if referring to food. It appears to be a Scottish variant of the early word *foison*, meaning 'plenty' or 'abundance'. There is also a word derived from it that I find quite appealing – *fushionless*, meaning 'lacking substance, strength, ineffective, weak'. One colourful 19th-century quote makes reference to 'these fushionless idlers'. Effective terms of abuse always come in handy, and if enough of you start using *fushionless* I can see it making something of a comeback. Even *fushion* has some uses. Both these words deserve a chance. Perhaps you could try slipping them into your next dinner party conversation – 'The food was tasty but lacking fushion', 'The performance was good, but where was the fushion?' The future success of *fushion* and *fushionless* – and don't forget *gry* – depends upon you!

As for the word that rhymes with *orange* – I don't believe there is one. Or perhaps someone could enlighten me here. Of course, if you allow the plural form, then a number of possibilities open up, one being *porringers* 'small bowls or basins from which porridge-like substances are eaten'. And the longest word in the language? Well, you'll just have to read *Blooming English* to find the answer to that one.

Bibliography

Allan, Keith and Burridge, Kate, *Euphemism and Dysphemism: Language used as Shield and Weapon*, Oxford University Press, New York, 1991.

Amherst, Alicia, *Children's Gardens*, Macmillan, London, 1902.

Andersson, Lars and Trudgill, Peter, *Bad Language*, Penguin Books, Harmondsworth, Middlesex, 1990.

Ayto, John, *A Gourmet's Guide: Food and Drink from A to Z*, Oxford University Press, Oxford, 1994.

Bierce, Ambrose, *The Devil's Dictionary*, Dover Publications, New York, [1911] 1993.

Blamires, Harry, *The Queen's English: The Essential Companion to Written English*, Bloomsbury, London, 1994.

Bolinger, Dwight, *Language: The Loaded Weapon*, Longman, Edinburgh Gate, Harlow, 1980.

Bradley, David, 'Regional Characteristics of Australian English Phonology' in Burridge, Kate and Bernd, Kortmann, *Varieties of English: The Pacific and Australasia*, Mouton de Gruyter, Berlin, 2005.

Burchfield, Robert, *The English Language*, Oxford University Press, Oxford, 1985.

— *New Fowler's Modern English Usage*, Oxford University Press, Oxford, 1996.

Burridge, Kate, *Blooming English: Observations on the Roots, Cultivation and Hybrids of the English Language*, Cambridge University Press, Cambridge, 2004.

Bybee, Joan, 'Mechanisms of Change in Grammaticization: The Role of Frequency' in Brian D. Joseph and Richard D. Janda (eds), *The Handbook of Historical Linguistics*, Blackwell, Oxford, 2003, pp. 602–23.

Cameron, Deborah, *Verbal Hygiene*, Routledge, London, 1995.

Craig, Alex, *Sex and Revolution*, Allen & Unwin, London, 1934.

Crystal, David, *The Cambridge Encyclopaedia of the English Language*, Cambridge University Press, Cambridge, 1995.

Cundall, Peter, *Seasonal Tasks for the Practical Australian Gardener,* Penguin Books, Ringwood, 1989.

Cutts, Martin and Maher, Chrissie, *Gobbledygook*, Allen & Unwin, London, 1984.

Earle, C W, *Pot-Pourri from a Surrey Garden*, Smith Elder and Co., London, 1897.

Elder, Bruce, *Blood on the Wattle: Massacres and Maltreatment of Australian Aboriginies since 1799*, Child & Associates, Frenchs Forest, NSW, 1988.

Ellis, Mary, *Growing and Using Herbs in Australia: Virtuous Weeds*, Little Hill Press, Crows Nest, NSW, 1995.

Ermert, Suzanne, *Gardener's Companion to Weeds*, New Holland Publishers, Sydney, 2001.

Fryer, Peter, *Mrs Grundy: Studies of English Prudery*, Dennis Dobson, London, 1963.

Grose, Francis, *Dictionary of the Vulgar Tongue*, London, [1783] 1811.

Heine, Bernd, *Cognitive Foundations of Grammar*, Oxford University Press, New York, 1997.

Hock, Hans Heinrich, *Principles of Historical Linguistics*, Mouton de Gruyter, Berlin, 1991.

Hock, Hans Heinrich and Joseph, Brian D, *Language History, Language Change, and Language Relationship*, Mouton de Gruyter, Berlin, 1996.

Horvath, Barbara, *Variation in Australian English: The Sociolects of Sydney*, Cambridge University Press, Cambridge, 1985.

Hughes, Geoffrey, *Words in Time*, Basil Blackwell, Oxford, 1988.

— *Swearing: A Social History of Foul Language, Oaths and Profanity in English*, Basil Blackwell, Oxford, 1991.

Jackson, Marie E, *The Florist's Manual,* Henry Colburn and Co, London, 1822.

Jacobsen, Anders, 'American political correctness and the word "niggardly"' in Blog, 3 September 2002, http://www.jacobsen.no/cgi-sys/cgiwrap/anders/MT/mt-tb.cgi/269

Jespersen, Otto, *A Modern English Grammar on Historical Principles: Part 1 (Sounds and Spelling)*, Allen & Unwin, London, 1961.

Kellaway, Deborah, *The Illustrated Virago Book of Women Gardeners*, Hodder and Stoughton, Rydalmere, NSW, 1997.

Lass, Roger, 'Phonology and Morphology' in Roger Lass (ed.), *The Cambridge History of the English Language*, Vol. 3 (1476–1776), Cambridge University Press, Cambridge, 1999.

Lockwood, Kim (ed.), *Style: A Guide for Journalists*, News Limited, Sydney, 2001.

Loftus, E F and Palmer J C, 'Reconstruction of Automobile Destruction: An Example of Interaction between Language and Memory', *Journal of Verbal Learning and Verbal Behaviour*, Vol. 13, 1974, pp. 585–89.

Loftus, E F, 'Leading Questions and the Eyewitness Report', *Cognitive Psychology*, Vol. 7, 1975, pp. 560–72.

Loury, Glenn C, 'Self-censorship', *Partisan Review*, Vol. 60, No. 4, 1993, pp. 608–18.

Mandelbaum, D B (ed.), *Selected Writings of Edward Sapir in Language, Culture and Personality*, University of California Press, Berkeley and Los Angeles, 1958.

Marshall, Jeremy and McDonald, Fred (eds), *Questions of English*, Oxford University Press, Oxford, 1994.

Merritt, Anna Lea, *An Artist's Garden*, George Allen & Sons, London, 1908.

Morris, William, *Hope and Fears for Art. Five Lectures Delivered in Birmingham, London and Nottingham 1878–1881*, Ellis & White, London, 1883.

Nares, R, *Elements of Orthoepy: Containing A Distinct View of the Whole Analogy of the English Language: So Far as it Relates to Pronunciation, Accent, and Quantity*, T. Payne, London, 1784.

Noonan, Peggy, 'Toward Candor and Courage in Speech' in Katherine Anne Ackley (ed.), *Essays from Contemporary Culture*, Harcourt Brace and Company, Fort Worth, 1998, pp. 368–76.

Nunberg, Geoffrey, 'What the usage panel thinks' in Christopher Ricks and Leonard Michaels (eds), *The State of the Language*, Faber and Faber, London, 1990, pp. 467–82.

O'Neil, Wayne, 'English Orthography' in Timothy Shopen and Joseph M. Williams (eds), *Standards and Dialects in English*,

Winthrop Publishers, Cambridge, Massachusetts, 1980, pp. 63–84.

Partridge, Eric, *Adventuring Among Words*, Andre Deutsch, London, 1961.

— *A Concise Dictionary of Slang and Unconventional English*, ed. Paul Beale, Routledge, London, 1991.

Peters, Pam, *The Cambridge Australian English Style Guide*, Cambridge University Press, Cambridge, 1995.

— *The Cambridge Guide to English Usage*, Cambridge University Press, Cambridge, 2004.

Pinker, Stephen, *The Language Instinct*, Penguin Books, Harmondsworth, Middlesex, 1994.

Pratt, Anne, *The Flowering Plants, Grasses, Sedges and Ferns of Great Britain*, Frederick Warne and Co, London, 1889.

Preston, Dennis R, 'The Story of Good and Bad English in the United States' in Watts and Trudgill (eds), *Alternative Histories of English*, Routledge, London, 2002, pp. 134–52.

Pyles, Thomas and Algeo, John, *The Origins and Development of the English Language*, Harcourt, Brace Jovanovich, Fort Worth, Texas, 1993.

Sackville-West, Vita, *A Joy of Gardening*, Harper & Brothers, New York, 1958.

Salisbury, Sir Edward, *The New Naturalist: Weeds and Aliens*, Collins, London, 1961.

Sapir, Edward, *Language*, Harcourt, New York, 1921.

Sindel, Brian (ed.), *Australian Weed Management Systems*, R G & F J Richardson, Melbourne, 2000.

Slobin, Dan I, *Psycholinguistics*, Scott, Foresman and Company, Illinois, 1970.

Stockwell, Robert and Minkova, Donka, *English Words: History and Structure*, Cambridge University Press, Cambridge, 2001.

Tannahill, Reah, *Food in History*, Penguin Books, Harmondsworth, Middlesex, 1988.

Tieken-Boon van Ostade, Ingrid, 'Robert Lowth and the Strong Verb System', *Language Sciences*, Vol. 24, 3–4, 2002, pp. 459–70.

Walker, J A, *Critical Pronouncing Dictionary and Expositor of the English Language*, G G J & J Robinson, London, 1791.

Wallis, J *Joannis Wallisii grammatical linguae anglicanae*, William Bowyer, London, 1653. (ed. and trans. J A Kemp as *John*

Wallis' Grammar of the English Language, Longman, London, 1972.)

Wilkins, David, *From Part to Person: Natural Tendencies of Semantic Change and the Search for Cognates*, Cognitive Anthropology Research Groups Working Paper 23, Max Planck Institute, Nijmegen, 1993.

Zachrisson, R E, 'Four hundred years of English spelling reform', *Studia Neophilologica*, Vol. 4, 1931.

List of interesting words